From the Start

Literally Literary Anthology, Volume I

Literally Literary Staff

Editors:

Heath Houston • Anna Rozwadowska • Indira Reddy

and Jessica Kaisk

visit us at
medium.com/literally-literary

Cover design: Heath Houston

ISBN: 9781088482360

CONTENTS

ACKNOWLEDGMENTS

Heath would like to thank his editors for making this possible. Good editors are hard to find, good editors who are also good friends? Well, if you find that, you damn well better hold on to it. Special thanks to my favorite Cub's fan for lighting my fire. Tha'll do.

Anna would like to thank her entire team: Heath and Indira, and acknowledge the work of Jess Kaisk in building such a wonderful publication. We work hard for our writers at Literally Literary, and I think it shows!

Indira would like to thank Heath, Anna and Jess for helping build LL while maintaining it as a fun, inspirational place to work. A special thanks to the writers whose talent makes LL possible.

Jess would like to thank all the readers and writers at LL for being a part of it and helping it grow, express heartfelt thanks to Heath for taking over so she could enjoy the birth and first years of her daughter's, and soon to be son's life, her husband, Michael, for indulging her every late night spent writing, talking with Heath, and making a sliver of a dream real.
Heath, we did it, you truly are the best!

FORWARD

Jess Kaisk started this little publication in 2015 with a fun name (*well, not exactly fun for **me** to try and say out loud, I seem to stumble over it every time*) and invited me to run it with her. Our goal was to promote literary writing in the face of the increasing dominance of "Reality TV" type writing, dry tech writing, and self-help. We wanted it to be a community of readers and writers, not just publishing, but encouraging, promoting, and bolstering writers, new and old alike.

Though ownership was later passed to me, it was Jess who started the ball rolling. I ran with that ball and together, she and I quickly gained over 20,000 readers from all over the world. This was not easy to manage but we made it work.

As time went by, life took its turns and twists and Jess was, eventually, unable to continue in an active manner. I ran things by myself for a while but the work got to be overwhelming (*especially since I run a few other publications, as well*) and so, I ventured into the unknown. With a heavy heart, I asked Jess to pass ownership over to me and then I took a gamble on some additional editors.

I can hardly come up with words for how lucky I got with Indira and Anna. Both are intelligent, dedicated, and hard-working, in addition to being true friends. I have to credit the both of them for Literally Literary finding new life. With their help, LL has experienced a level of activity unseen prior, and we recently had the pleasure of watching our readership pass 25,000!

If things weren't positive enough, Jess rejoined the editor staff! She was always going to be a part of LL, but to have her back and active, well, that's a hell of a way to kick off this book.

And so, it is with a heart full of love and appreciation that I introduce you to the first Literally Literary Anthology, *From the Start*. May it be the first of many.

WE ARE NOT LOST

Heath Houston

As blinders of black fall,
remember the dawn
remember it starts again, clean,
it always starts again
and we are not the end
no, even when it feels like we are a cliff,
we are not the end

We give tears to the night
and push through to dawn
where it starts again, clean,
it always starts again
and we are not the last
though, god help me, it feels that way
we are not the last

The burning in you, in me,
still lingers in us at dawn
but we start again, clean,
we always start again
and we are not lost
no, just not quite found enough yet, but,
love, we are not lost.

THE BRIDGE OF LOST SOULS
Indira Reddy

We met for the first time on the Bridge of Lost Souls, twenty years ago to the very day. In those days, I believed in the Gods and in our lore. That's what drew me here — the possibility of one final goodbye to Kara. Oh! I forgot. You're new here, right? And you don't know me.

Please forgive an old woman for her wandering mind.

Lachlan returned the old woman's gentle smile with his own warm one. She looked so frail, so harmless…but the rumours he'd heard about her, echoed in his mind. He needed to find out her story, find something that would spark his sulking Muse to be what She once was…

We were talking about the Gods. *When the Gods first built this world, they gave one species, us humans, the soul.* And what an underhanded blow that was! On one hand, our souls gave us beauty and philosophy and poetry, and on the other, was the possibility of an eternity in unrest. You see, we believe that the souls of anyone who died in sleep remain in this world, instead of slowly dissipating to nothing. Horrifying, isn't it?

To remain in this world, without the capacity to touch anyone or anything, just being…in a half-asleep state. There was one loophole though. Everyone loves the idea of salvation, right? Heh!

What was I saying? Oh, yes. Every year, on the summer solstice, when the day is long and warm, if a loved one of the person who died comes to the Bridge of Souls and calls out, their voice could wake the half-asleep soul; who would, warmed by the long day, be the nearest to awakening that they'd ever be. And if the voice was loud enough and their love strong enough, the soul would wake up, understand that the body is dead and give itself up to nothing. You can see this happening sometimes. There's a burst of purple light that slowly fades to grey and then disappears. Here's the best part — with the thousands of people who throng this bridge on the summer solstice, there's no way of knowing whose voice reached whose soul; there's only faith that it was who you came for. Faith! Pah!

Lachlan smiled at her vehemence. He too had little time for faith; he only believed in verifiable things.

Once, I believed too…believed that my voice would reach Kara's, that my beautiful baby would not suffer…I believed until the day I saw that purple light disappear right in front of me, ten years ago. I had been calling out to Kara for the past four hours when a soul appeared in front of me. It had to be her. Finally!

I was drowning in happiness and remorse when I noticed her. She was standing next to me, almost in a trance, sparkling tears flowing ceaselessly, a beatific smile. A few minutes after the light disappeared completely, she sighed and visibly shook herself. She turned to me and wished me luck and that I could feel the same peace she was feeling. I was astounded since the light was Kara. I told her that. She shook her head softly, patted my arm consolingly and said that the light spoke to her in her husband's voice, the husband who died last year while in a coma. Then, she walked away.

I was furious. She was trying to take my Kara and make her into something, someone else. I wasn't going to stand for it, but neither could I do anything here. So, I followed her home, made her recant her lies with my fists and left her leaking red all over her pristine soft yellow carpet.

Lachlan's eyes widened at this confession. He wondered why someone hadn't arrested her already.

That night, I went to bed, certain that with the dissipation of Kara's soul, I wouldn't have to face that nightmare again. But, it came, as piercingly sharp as ever, each microsecond stretched to minutes — my hand raised in anger for the hundredth time; her eyes blazing defiance, her stance hardening; my fury increasing — *because she never understood how I was doing this for her own good;* her feet tripping as my fist deformed the soft fat of her stomach; the almost inaudible whoosh of breath as her whole body tensed with pain; my tears — *I hated causing her pain, but she wouldn't be normal and if I didn't punish her and Gods forbid, if she started liking her abnormality, the horror of it all was unspeakable;* her hand reaching out automatically to steady herself but slipping; the way her head hit the floor and bounced back like a rubber ball; her momentary fainting. Fast forward to the next day, when she lay in her bed, dead. The Gods were very cruel, snatching her away before she got a chance to be who she could be.

Lachlan shivered in the warm sun as it dawned on him that the old woman still believed that she had been doing the right thing, that her daughter's death was a trick of fate rather than her own doing.

That's when I knew that the light hadn't been Kara. Maybe it was that woman's husband after all. I went back to the bridge the next year.

"And the woman?" prompted Lachlan, "the woman whose husband might have been the soul you saw."

She died. I am pretty thorough and I didn't want to waste my life behind bars, so… I continued visiting the bridge. Every year, I saw the purple light and every year someone else claimed it. I fought them for their claim, first with my fists, then with my stick and finally with my poison. Age, you see, creeps up on a person and you have to adapt to it.

"No one found out about you all those years?" asked Lachlan.

No. Not until that bastard Grigol appeared.

A flash of lightning shattered the bright blue sky. The rumbling thunder resonated with fury as the old woman laughed aloud. For the first time in his life, Lachlan felt fear animating his whole body. His brain, the primitive lizard part of it, screamed at him in panic. He froze as the old woman spoke to the sky.

You're just a jumped-up human with superpowers, Grigol. What are you going to do? Turn me to ash? Do it. Release me. Don't worry, young man. Grigol's not going to do anything. He hates being cursed at, so I do it to him all the time.

"*Grigol is one of the Gods,*" *said Lachlan,* "*and you curse him?*"

Everyone needs some entertainment, right. Plus, he's the one who ratted me out to the police. He appeared in a dream to one of the big ones, commissioner, I think and arranged a sting operation. They caught me with my needle deep into that woman's arm.

"*But you're not in jail. How's that possible?*" *asked Lachlan.*

It's that stupid Grigol again. He appeared in court and cursed me. Every day except the solstice, I have to walk to this bridge and stand here waiting for a few hours. On the day of the solstice, I sleep. No matter how many uppers I swallow, on that day, I sleep. The court felt that was an appropriate punishment, that death and dissipation were too good for me.

Thunder rumbled without lightning, almost as if someone were laughing. "*So, you stopped killing,*" *said Lachlan.*

Stopped? Why would I?

A needle glinted as the old woman lunged for him. Lachlan jumped. The needle grazed his clothes. Without a word, he started running. The woman's cold laughter followed him, echoing in his ears

DEFECTIVE
Matt Vercillo

I watched
a goose break
from formation
turn around and
head due north.
Alone,
defective, free.

And I, the idiot
on the ground
saw meaning
where there was
only madness
and certain death.

I AM IN THE STARS
Marika Bianca

do you think of me
in the hollow still of night
when the heavyhearted world's gone silent and black

do you stare at the unkind ceiling
and replay the fateful memory of our past
our pantomime in heartbreak

do you long for me
and ache
for what might have been

do you feel the salty sting of tears
when you see me in your mind's eye
hurt

do you look in the mirror and see something
missing

do you make love to her and feel my breath on your neck
my fingers in your hair
my lips on your chest

do you look through her
and see me

do you remember what I taste like

do you crave me like I crave you

do you feel me
falling

do you feel my starved tears
drowning

can you hear me whispering

I love you

I love you

look for me in the heavens tonight

I am in the stars
punching through the dark sky of what we lost

GAMAYUN AND THE LEVIATHAN
Michael Stang

No love as strong hath brought the heavens' keep to bear her
salvaged duty.

In gilded perspicuity, revelation across the land, she searches for
the one who does not know he draws her star from the night's sky,
ever towards the cross unity.

A crystal protectorate of wisdom, seer of all creation, a messenger,
Gamayun's aura bundles the hunter's heart ready for the journey.

The path lay gory in slaughterer's field, sward covered ancient
bone,
her map towards insinuated proof where he is rumored to lay
prone.

She threw her body to the transparent sharpened pace, the swift
she will fly towards the depth of him. Without their bodies
impetus brew, coagulated base, there lies no purpose no renew.

> Exhort his devils, you healer. Enter his hall of
> wretched Abyss.
> For there be rules written long ago; love is balance
> You must equal his evil to conjure bliss.

Spawned of titans evil brood Leviathan scoured the darkness
through,
great fathoms of sea, obstinate chaos insanity did he oil ocean's

death-plague.

Haughty breath execrated holy might against all takers,
severed heads in watery cells contained.

Steep legacy the climb of body mounts, there are no sounds of life
only the slough of his muscle wreathed tail
ruthless barbs renewed, diamonds tapered to a petrified edge,
once more whipped on every side
to cut what remained.

Fear struck the elemental — *time his immortal enemy.*
A deity from above, wrath soaked pike in hand, flushed the seas
and drained his stash hoard away.
For all he could he could not without tides, slithered in mud til
turned desert fray.
Thunderbolt angels' speculation advanced along his flanks,
no longer able he rolled on his back and flared a diabolical soul
coiled within his belly, beyond all sessions of reality and
expectation.

Left for Osiris' worms, they cut his wings — hectares from his
tail.
Oh sorcerer's pride dug with his head and pulled what was left
out of the blistered path of sun, to a leaked crypt under the last
cataract trinket dot of cool — *death's final nail.*

To close these eyes that have seen damnation, to leave them be.
He thought to close those weary eyes forever … forever, such a
sweet song.
And there at last the piercing start apocalyptic heart
butterflied the brute's wrong.

Vapor queries escapes the traveled sphere to race the life lines
down to her mate.
Gamayun lets her hunter fly, arrow straight and true into that
twitching, seething mass.
All went silent, the lizard still, the queen of knowing thought
herself too late.

She ran to him gently. Holds the monsters' broken head in arms.
she cuddles blossom's agony.

By his ear the midnight maiden tells him of earthen fair and soft
forest air, of her thighs and rear, wildflower deep ravines breathes
the future and what gods she will birth by their joining of their
salts.

Keeper of the beginning sheds epiphanic tears.
From Moscow fields to Belarus peaks to the mythical east she
cries.

Eddies to pools rivers to lakes, to seas the waterfalls comply.
The land reshapes, gathers it's boon, for a thousand years
the fountainhead stays the Devil of this wound.

> One a silver tear one a crumpled mass, they
> kept the river's flow, mankind's love to pass.

LITTLE RED RIDES AGAIN

Sometimes, a girl's gotta do what a girl's gotta do
Elle Fredine

I knew as soon as I saw him step down from the stage-coach, he was trouble. The stink of it clung to him in the smell of stale sweat from his travel-stained clothes. I could see it in the way he pushed through the swinging doors and stalked over to the bar. I could read it in the tension of his gloved hand as he raised the glass of whiskey to his narrow-lipped gash of a mouth.

His squinty, blood-shot eyes darted around, taking in the room quickly, but without seeming to notice anything in particular.

Only two kinds of men size up a room like that — stupid ones running towards trouble, and frightened ones running away from it.

I moved a little further down the bar, wiping my cloth over long-dried spills and old stains, and wondered which he'd turn out to be.

He tossed his drink back, grimaced as it went down. I wasn't offended. We don't run to fancy liquor. Not much call for it. He set his glass on the counter, then fished in his vest for a coin and plunked it down beside his glass — a gold double eagle.

I sidled over to refill his glass. "Don't sell anythin' costs that much, friend."

The corner of his mouth twitched and curled. More of a snarl than a smile, but then, a real smile wouldn't have sat right on his craggy, pock-marked face. It sure never reached those flat, black eyes. Two smooth stones, they were. Predator's eyes.

In spite of the heat, I shivered.

Across the narrow, rutted street, their boots echoing on the raised boardwalk, two kids ran, laughing, into Farley's Mercantile.

The man turned at their noise, pushed his Stetson back and stared after them.

I wondered what we must look like to him. A bunch of down-at-the-heels townies who'd prob'ly never amount to much, trying to eke out a living near the border. A cluster of clapboard houses with peeling paint. No more'n a pimple on the butt-end of the world.

A few hard-scrabble farms. A dozen scruffy, cash-poor ranches. A general store with a funeral parlour in the back. A bank so small nobody's ever been tempted to rob it.

The church does duty as meeting hall and courthouse, as well as a school for the town's half-dozen kids. Marry 'em, teach 'em and tax 'em all in the same place. Efficient, at least.

Just like every other dusty little town on the edge of the desert where the stage only stops once a week. A place most sensible people would blow right through along with the tumbleweeds.

The late afternoon sun blazed white-hot through the smeared, fly-specked windows flanking the swinging, saloon doors. Time to pull the shades down. Maybe draw the wooden shutters part-way. Give the regulars some respite from the heat. They were nursing their drinks at a table near the end of the bar, as far from the door as they could get.

I s'pose I should've closed 'em earlier, the shutters, but to be honest, I really don't mind the heat.

The stranger's expressionless gaze returned to my face. "I'm looking for some old friends. Might be they passed through here a while back."

I polished a shot glass and thought hard. "Your friends got names?"

The man placed his thumb on the twenty-dollar gold piece. He raised his voice so the fellas clustered around the back table could hear. "Or might be my friends're still here."

Ol' Rafe Pruitt, his grizzled beard stained from the tobacco plug he habitually chewed, swiveled around on his chair and eyed the stranger up and down. Then he pushed his hat back and carefully mopped his wrinkled forehead with his red neckerchief.

He levelled a stream of brown juice at the spittoon near the bar. It missed and hit the floor, spattering up little clumps of sawdust. Rafe shrugged and turned back to his cronies.

The stranger stiffened. His hand dropped to his side and hovered over the butt of the well-polished Colt he wore low-slung and tied down. A gunslinger's rig.

Then his shoulders relaxed. The little half-smile, half-snarl touched his mouth again. "You got a gunsmith?"

"Lookin' to buy a new piece?" I nodded towards Farley's. "He'll be in soon. Mr. Farley an' his missus — every Friday for my beef stew and biscuits. House special." I nodded to the hand-lettered sign behind the bar. Room 50 cents, Bath 50 cents, Meals 50 cents, Clean sheets 1 dollar.

The stranger read the sign. His lips twitched. "His wife a red-head? Name of Annabelle?"

Out of the corner of my eye, I seen Ol' Rafe straighten up. He slipped out of his chair and sidled out the back door, real casual. I was pretty sure the stranger noticed, too, though he didn't let on.

"Nossir, I believe her name's Mary-Louise."

The stranger slid the double eagle across the counter to me. Pulled a tattered paper from his pocket and unfolded it. On it was a blurry image of a woman in a cloak, along with several men. "Wanted for Bank Robbery. $5000. Annabelle "Little Red" Pennebaker and the Notorious Pennebaker Gang."

A bounty hunter. I stared at the picture, aware of his eyes on me. "Could be anybody."

The stranger shrugged and re-folded the paper. Tucked it away in his vest.

My hand hovered over the coin. "You'll be wantin' a room and a bath?"

"Might be."

I opened my mouth to ask if he wanted supper, too, when Matt Farley came strollin' across the narrow street with Mary-Louise on his arm.

Normally, I'd'a been pleased. Those two can light up a room just by walkin' in. Matt's a tall, good-lookin' devil, but

Mary-Louise… You can see she's real quality, even in her plain, gingham dress and poke-bonnet. Sparklin' grey eyes, pale skin the sun never seems to touch and a mass of auburn curls she braids tight and coils around her head.

Their two little boys, one dark like Matt, the other the spit an' image of Mary-Louise, came clatterin' after them.

Matt took one look at the stranger and gathered Mary-Louise and the boys close. He said something real quiet-like in her ear I didn't catch. Her chin tilted up and she shook her head, 'no'. Matt scowled but led the way to a table by the windows.

Supper was a quiet affair. Word of the bounty hunter must've got 'round pretty fast, 'cause most of the townsfolk seemed to've found better ways to spend their evening. A few trickled in. After a glance or two at the stranger, they ate quietly and left. Some exchanged a few words with the Farleys.

The setting sun cast a golden glow over the handsome little family at the table by the window, silhouetting them against a backdrop of flame-streaked clouds.

It was one of those rare, magical desert sunsets most city folks never get to see. As the sky faded from scarlet to orange and finally a deep, dusky purple, long shadow-fingers crept across the low hills behind town. A couple of coyotes yammered in the arroyo back of the saloon.

The stranger stood quiet the whole time, his back to the light, sipping his liquor, watching the family's reflection in the fly-spotted mirror hanging behind the bar.

Finally, they finished eating. Matt Farley pushed back his chair and walked over to the bar.

I poured him a drink and moved away.

He raised his glass and nodded to the stranger's reflection. "Evenin'."

The stranger's eyes glimmered. His mouth twitched in that snarling grimace again and he lifted his glass. "Evenin'."

"Hot day for travelin'." Matt's gaze took in the stranger's appearance from his worn, hand-tooled boots to the crown of his dusty, black Stetson. "You come far?"

"Fair piece."

Matt finished his drink and set the glass on the bar. He studied the stranger's hawk-nosed profile and nodded again. "Safe journey."

The man never moved while the Farleys shepherded their boys off home. As their footsteps died away on the boardwalk, the stranger removed his Stetson and scrubbed a hand through his shock of sandy hair.

I refilled his glass. He pulled another double-eagle from his vest pocket and set it on the bar. "Leave the bottle." He nodded towards the coin. "I'll take that room, now. Make sure to use the clean sheets."

I placed the key to Number Three on the bar. "It's ready for you. Up the stairs, first door on your left."

He drained his glass and set it on the bar, stared at the key for a moment. "I believe I'll go for a walk, first. Mebbe take in the sights." Holding the bottle by the neck, he strode into the night.

Half-past midnight and the cramped hayloft in the livery stable was still stifling from the heat of the day. A handful of chaff itched its way down my back. The straw under my belly smelled old and musty and prickled through my shirt. Shouldn't 'a left my apron at the saloon.

Soft light from the crescent moon riding low on the horizon filtered through cracks and chinks between the warped boards, casting bars of pale silver across the inky shadows below.

The pole ladder creaked under the weight of a dark figure. A head appeared above the railing. My finger tensed on the trigger of my sawed-off, Remington twelve-gauge.

The head turned to the right and then the left, scanning the loft; silent and stealthy as a Lobo wolf, watching for its prey to twitch.

I closed my eyes, barely breathing. Forced my hand to relax. One… two… three…

The head withdrew.

Footsteps sounded below. Hinges groaned as the huge double doors swung open.

"Bounty-man." The word sliced through the warm night, sharp as a Bowie knife.

"Annabelle Pennebaker … thought I'd never catch up with you."

"It's Farley. Missus Matthew Farley."

"I see you brought reinforcements. Looks like the whole gang's here."

I raised my head, careful not to make any noise. Matt and Mary-Louise stood in the doorway, dressed for travel.

Under a short-waisted, corduroy jacket, Matt's flannel shirt was tucked into wool pants. His Stetson was pulled low. A large, red neckerchief, knotted loose, hung down his shirt-front under his long, heavy cotton duster.

Mary-Louise had traded her gingham for a divided riding skirt in soft doe-skin and matching, long-sleeved shirt, topped off with a dark, woolen cloak. The hood was thrown back, its red silk lining framing her pale face.

Old Rafe Pruit and half the townsfolk flanked them in a loose semi-circle, all with long dusters and red neckerchiefs, same as Matt. Most carried repeating rifles or smooth-bores. Ready to ride. Nobody moved. Nobody spoke.

They watched the man from the saloon — the bounty hunter.

Matt took a couple of steps to one side, widening the gap between himself and Mary-Louise. He tucked his duster back, revealing a pair of tied-down Colts. "The way I see it, you have two choices."

The bounty hunter chuckled and angled himself towards Matt. "Which one of you to shoot before the other drops me?"

"You can leave. Right now. Ride out and forget you were ever here." Mary-Louise's rich contralto was cold as an icy wind off the Sierra Madres.

"Or?"

"Or, you can die here."

The bounty hunter's mouth lifted in a wolfish grin. He moved slowly towards Matt. "My, my, Miz Pennebaker, You're a long way from those Kansas City saloons. But I think life in this backwater's made you soft. Offering me a way out? I think I like my chances…" He broke off — whipped around quick as a rattler and dove towards Mary-Louise.

Twin Colts bloomed in Matt's hands as the thunder of a forty-five calibre shattered the air.

The bounty-man doubled over and dropped hard, face-down.

Matt stalked over and prodded the huddled, motionless form with the toe of his boot. He stuck his foot under the man's chest and lifted. The bounty hunter rolled over in a boneless sprawl, arms out-flung, sightless eyes stretched wide. A crimson puddle was already spreading from the bullet-hole dead-center in his chest.

"Dammit, Red." Matt holstered his pistols and glared at his wife.

She shrugged. "I'll be slower next time — and it's Mary-Louise, remember?" She holstered her still-smoking pistol and tucked her arm through Matt's. "C'mon, cowboy. Let's go home."

Me'n Ol' Rafe trundled the bounty hunter's body past the church to the tiny graveyard at the edge of town. The shovels we'd tucked in the wheelbarrow alongside him rattled and clanked as we bumped across the wagon ruts and into the fenced patch of stony, hallowed ground

We stood for a minute, sweating in the cool breeze rolling down from the hills. Ol' Rafe sniffed the air like a hound-dog scentin' a rabbit. "Be cooler soon. Already snowin' in the mountains."

"Best get to digging." My shovel thudded into the hard-pack. "Damn, this is gonna take a while."

I heard a glugging sound beside me. Ol' Rafe wiped his mouth on his cuff and passed over a whiskey bottle. "Raise one for the dearly departed?"

I caught the gleam of teeth and grinned back. "Don't mind if I do. Shame to waste liquor."

We were sweatin' hard by the time we'd dug the hole deep enough. I s'pose we could'a left him for the coyotes, but even the meanest dog deserves a decent burial.

I wondered if more would follow. Five thousand dollars is a lot of money. But then, I realized the notion was too absurd for

most folks. Who'd ever imagine a notorious gang of outlaws —
bank robbers — would retire to this dust-bowl? A whole town-
full of 'em? Led by a red-headed, gunslingin' woman in a scarlet
hood?

As we rolled the bounty hunter into the hole and set up his
marker, I had to chuckle. "No, siree — nobody'd ever believe it,
that's for sure."

INHIBITIONS

Anna Rozwadowska

One crushes watermelon seeds, not the heart,
not the heart what in humanity tears us apart, so?

What genius of mind atmospheres of dissolution from love,
transcendence of mind, energy swirling between beings moving
the dance of lovers and thinkers alike, philosophers and writers
alike,

what tears us apart?

Words and intentions define the human race,
the space stands still if we see no more beauty of one's face,
returns innocence to the skies, relinquish your control beast,
let humanity become what it needs to be: perfectly free...

I am with thee, with thee,
my soul sets me free, my inhibitions set me free,
I am the river that moves free beneath the golden sun,
while you run, you run.

Tell yourself a tale of what once was, for you lived your scenario,
loved exchanging minds, written stories from two hearts,
the very things that tears us apart; set yourself free, move towards
me,

flower, intricate be,
you are you and you are me,
we are essence, essentially.

Let not our glow dissipate beneath the sun, *I am one, you are one,*
come to me under the sun,
fear be gone I am lore and you; the escape of my being,
creating together splendid pleasure.

Refuse the quarrel, give into me, I hold you so very tight,
refuse your might, it senses your longing let go into me,
set yourself free, age not in this world ephemeral between stars,
what we lost no longer applies,
I am the joy that escapes you, you are the fine line between the
skies,
I am alright with losing myself,
If you join me,

right,

now.

THE WOMEN IN MY STORIES
Rebeca Ansar

these fingers will write fiction
about colored bodies,
about female bodies

peripheralized due only
to their darkness,
to their womanness

their tales will allude to histories
willfully forced aside in our education
to dedicate more space for the colonizer's
repeated, regurgitated, lionization

a jarring reflection of lived experience

their names will be unfamiliar at first
but, if we let our tongues rehearse them

we will find a mellifluousness
that has been suppressed
for longer than we
have breathed freely,

and perhaps, a part of us
will be released alongside
their stories.

THROUGH THE LIGHT

LB

Still are the days in these wooden cabins
Loved are the strong trees along the road
Curious are the boats adrift in blue water
Protected are the clouds in sheltered skies
Loved are the ones who listen to the wind
Grateful are the eyes that follow the light

CLOUDY DAYS
Jess Kaisk

My mind is blank,
an empty page
waiting…

The winds gust in
leaves twirling
a lusty gale…

I wonder about things,
where the wind goes
who sings to the trees
why the clouds are grey
like my mood
why do we have moods

My mind remains blank
words scattered by a
Northern wind
glacial kisses on my skin
pages ripped from frozen fingers

HELIOTROPIC

Guérin Asante

How can this not
be a rhythm
much like every maple
finger, red revealing
one by one
on never less than
a million tender arms?

How is it not
as near as our feet, through
those which keep
their inflorescence and uplift
themselves with
every beat of vapor?

I have had to bury
every shape of seed above
the place
our oldest play
with coal;

I watch them
see themselves
as diamonds, looking back

into their former bones
blue-green
and incandescent —

*Tell me — how could
these hours not be*

but a dance

TRANSACTIONS
Ambrose Hall

There is 53p in change on the bedside table, which is all
we have left. The yellowed wallpaper curls at the corner above my
head and threatens to peel off. The damp patch has spread across
the sloping section of the attic roof, creating an intricate pattern of
greenish flowers. It's doing a better job of creating than Paul, who
has given up staring at a blank canvas for the day and is now
slumped in our one chair — a tubular steel thing we pulled from
a skip — smoking out of the propped-open window.

The sheets I lie on are sticky, musty. They adhere to my
bare skin. I unstick them, pull myself up off the bed, swaying a
little, empty bottle still in one hand. The drink dulls the insistent
hunger chewing at my insides.

"I suppose I'd better go and see one of my gentlemen," I
say… slur. I'll sober up soon enough.

He doesn't even have the decency to protest. We'd agreed I
wouldn't have to do this again, but that was weeks ago. Such
promises are no longer our currency.

"You're a fucking washout," I say louder, hoping for a
reaction. I stagger and he flinches, as if I might throw the bottle at
him. I make a point of setting it down carefully on the side.

I pull on trousers, a thick jumper, a long coat. My clothes
swamp me, but I can't stand to go out in the cold in any less. I've
no fat left on my bones and the wind whips right through me.

Paul's eyes are on me, watching me move around the flat. I
know that. I take a little extra time, waiting for him to ask.

He doesn't.

Well, fuck his pride. Others will.

Out on the street, I dial Jimmy Bergsen's number and he

picks right up.

"You working on a case, Jimmy?" I ask.

"Always. I thought you retired."

"I thought so, too. Seems I was wrong."

"You know I can always use a little inspiration. Usual rates?"

"I'll be over in five."

Jimmy's office is in an old block that should have been torn down years ago. Half of it is vacant. Place must have some powerfully eccentric landlord to still be standing. Its age doesn't lend it any character, or if it does, it's the kind you don't want to meet on a dark night. His building is built of dark brown brick, giving it a grubby, depressed air that's only compounded by the dirt which sticks to it. Many of the windows are boarded up and the boards papered over with old gig posters forming a papier mâché layer. Inside is no better. The walls are inlaid with a sort of worn down grey-brown wood that's so ingrained with dirt, you can smell it. Goes right up my nose when I step inside. In the centre, running up the middle, is one of those old cage lifts. The central hall needs light, and that compounds the general grubbiness, the dimness of it all.

Jimmy Bergsen is waiting for me in his office when I climb from the metal death trap that somehow sees me to his floor in one piece. He's a big square guy — broad shoulders, wide jaw, nose that's been pounded into his face one too many times and decided to stay there. Looks a little too much like his Viking ancestors, save the shabby grey suit, which doesn't fit, in every sense.

"You okay, kid? You're looking thin." He rubs his hands together, rubs the back of his neck. He's not looking too well himself these days, vivid pink skin hinting at a blood pressure problem. But Jimmy always did work too hard.

"I'm just fine, Jimmy," I say, slipping my coat off onto one of his chairs. "Times have been a little lean of late, is all."

He hurries to lock his office door, so I lose my jumper and

shirt, as well. Pile them all up on the chair and stand naked in the middle of his office. He comes up behind me, curls one large hand around my ribcage.

"Why don't you tell me about your case," I say, while his hands relearn the shapes of my body. It's been a while.

"I don't like seeing you like this."

I shrug. I'm not here for a personal connection. I know he'd take me in, just like Paul took me in. They all make promises, but in the end, it's the same old same old. I burn a little too bright for them and they pull their fingers away, disgusted by our transactions in the final analysis.

His hands rest on my hips, or what's left of my hips. The bone juts out painfully and I know he'll be thinking that.

"Can I at least take you out for a meal afterwards?" he asks.

"All right."

"All right. Good. *Jesus.* I thought you said he was going to take care of you."

"Jimmy," I say with a sigh. "Are we doing this or not?"

He steps round in front of me, runs a hand across my shoulder. He closes his eyes, breathes. His fingers leave a trace of gold across my skin. A little of the old magic.

"My client lost her daughter. An addict, but that didn't kill her. My client thinks there was a cover up, but that's just a hunch. The police were investigating and then: nothing, silence."

"And what do you think?"

His hands follow the lines of my body, down to my thighs. Linger there, unsure whether to continue. "I think she has a point." His voice is low, barely above a whisper, as if he's saying something deeply erotic to me. Sweet nothings, instead of a murder case. "I'm getting nowhere with my usual contacts. Something isn't right."

It's been a while since Jimmy has used my services and he seems to need a little help getting up the nerve. I find his hand with mine, move it across to the blank space between my legs and leave it there.

His hand is shaking as his fingers trace a line up my pelvis, leaving a seam of warmth behind which splits. White light spills from the crack as it widens, as it grows up my abdomen, following his fingers, spreading in a jagged line up the centre of my chest.

I hold my arms out, palms up, in invitation. The light from within me illuminates Jimmy's dim office in a brilliant burst, coaxing vibrant colours from the faded decor. "Do it!" I urge.

Jimmy forces his thumbs inside my chest cavity, cracks me open with his big meaty hands and climbs inside. His bulk fills me to bursting, forcing up inside my throat like choking, stretching me to fingertips and toes. My skin and flesh stretch thin to surround him, cover him over, seal him in. He gibbers within me — details of his case, name and numbers, the minutiae whirring round his brain, absorbing my light and energy. Traces of his impressions mix with my thoughts: the mother's face, the daughter's, Jimmy's police contacts, their blank eyes, dead ends. I feel the whir of his mind, the click as of a machine starting up.

Yes. Yes. He has it.

He strains against the edges of my body, until he finds purchase on my skin, breaks a hole in me with one nail, tears.

I crouch on the floor, spilling all over the grey lino, Jimmy beside me shaking. "There's some personal connection between the police and the killer," he pants. "Someone trying to protect their relation. I know it."

I pull my skin together, seal up the door he left in me until I'm whole again. Feel the flesh of my body, firmer now, some padding on my bones. I stand, pull on clothes and catch my reflection in the glass of his office door — the hollows of my eyes, my cheeks, a little less desperate, a little more fashionable. Not enough, but it's a start.

Jimmy's eyes are on me. I see the calculation in them as he takes on the results of our transaction. He looks away. It's always in this moment they feel it. The drop. Not what I've given, but what I've taken. They wonder if they can spare it. They wonder what sort of creature I am.

I have no answer.

I take the envelope of cash he's left on the desk and leave silently. He won't want to take me to dinner. They never do.

I take a taxi across town, stop for a drink in the bar at the end of the street — a quick whisky I knock back to take the edge off before I return to the attic, to Paul. As an afterthought, I buy a bottle from the off-licence. The hunger will be back soon enough.

This scene is getting old. I climb the three flights of stairs to the attic, and they ghost beneath me, all the stairs I have climbed, all the garrets I've lived in, the mouldy hovels, the remote cottages. All the scenes of desperation, the grasping of every man who's wanted my gift and resented me after. Always the same story. They want me scooped out, emptied. They want a one way street.

Paul is slumped on the floor when I enter, his once white t-shirt greyish with dirt, his face smeared with something that isn't paint. Cigarette ash? It wouldn't be the first time I've walked in on a dead lover, but no, Paul is only wishing for it.

My phone rings. It's Jimmy.

"I'm sorry about earlier," he says.

I make an unspecific noise in response.

"I called one of my contacts, pressed him a little harder. Turns out the Chief Inspector has a half-brother with some unfortunate habits. My contact asked me to hush it up, said they're dealing with it internally. I told him to go fuck himself. The mother deserves some answers, don't you think?"

"That's great, Jimmy." I don't bother to put much enthusiasm into it. They always seem to need their pat on the head from me. I'll never understand why.

"Thanks, kid. I owe you one."

Jimmy's a practical man. They always bounce back the quickest. Not like Paul. Paul can wallow for days, blending his doubt with self-loathing into something toxic and redirecting it at me. He's a real artist in that regard.

I slip my phone into my pocket and watch Paul wake and rise, shuffle over to the bed and sit on the edge, staring at a canvas of me silhouetted in an archway. One of the first he painted, when he still appreciated my gift. He'd stayed up all night in ecstasy, forming my naked image across the canvas as though I'd burned it into him. As though it still burned and only painting it could give him relief. The drop hadn't come until the next day when he'd stood staring at his work, *our* work, eyes wide like a lost child and I saw the end had begun.

"I'm leaving tomorrow," I say. I can't survive like this. He knows and doesn't care. "One more time, for old time's sake?" I add, as an afterthought. I'd like to go out of here with a little more flesh on my bones.

After a few moments he turns, nods. After weeks of resisting, he finally gives up his qualms. Abandons some last claim to whatever passes for dignity in his little world.

He hauls himself up from the bed, comes over to me as I shed my clothes in a puddle at my feet.

"Tell me about your work," I say.

His fingers rest on my ribcage and he studies them there, the dirt beneath his nails where paint used to be, the yellow pads of nicotine stains between his index and middle finger. He closes his eyes and traces a line across my stomach, leaving a trail of gold in his wake.

TOUCH STARVED
Indira Reddy

Two weeks in a new town
and I'm starved…

I wish
I want
I desire
I need

today, right now

to feel a touch
a touch without expectations
a touch that is intentional
a touch without a smarmy grin behind it
a touch that is just simple contact

human to human

a touch that says hi
a touch that says I understand
a touch that says I feel your pain
a touch that says you're not alone

from one human to another

a touch of friendship
of compassion
of humanity

Just a single touch
so I know that I am alive
and not drifting in shadowy dreams
so I know that I haven't lost
the ability to feel

just a single simple human touch

MOTHER
Existence

the velvet-lined womb
shielding me from what I wasn't aware of
I set my heart on running free
yet the prison never permitted me
the cords that were deemed as bars
sealing me
from what, again?

she whispered the fairytales
but I yearned to wrap myself around them
her words flowed like the river
but I desired to glimpse the ocean

veiled between the princesses
were the customary perils of the world
she strived to apprise me
subtly
but all I made out were the chirps of the hummingbirds, calling
out to me
in reality, they fluttered off when advanced towards
I suppose they heretofore grasped the perfidy thrust into the books
singing didn't usher the mice to sew my dress
hence she did it.

oh, mother!
why weren't you louder?
why didn't you inform me concerning the sweet boy
waiting to withdraw my innocence,

why didn't you inform me that fire isn't just a radiant source on
snowy days
but a measure of inflicting torment on maidens who merely
render a cup of water to the seemingly forlorn,
why didn't you inform me that my skin had the option of
persisting as exclusively mine
no one else's.
why did you use the story of little red riding hood to compel my
cognition
the cruelty of misconception
for I only listened to the part regarding the *berries,*
and I granted the wolf in
perceiving him to be my savior

I would've lingered in there
for more than nine mere months
had I known that that was the solitary concealed whereabout
I would've declared I required further time
that I wasn't prepared.

here and now
I sit in the shreds of my felicity
if I close my eyes
if I consume the dreamland you long before flaunted
I don't desire to see his face, *no,*
I desire to be transported into your strong embrace
one I searched for in *every man*
but only remember it emerging from you

thus I'm proceeding to *close my eyes*
no one shall disturb me
for I'm getting my Mother back

RÊVERIES
Giovanni Sonier

The jetting lifeblood
of zestful green flesh,
the crux of her heart,
perpetually pumping
a bottomless blue
in your babbling brooks,
constantly making rounds
and rounds 'round
your nooks and curves,
splashing, soaking, sousing
your innards with a sweet
varnish-clear Adam's ale,
that which inflames
early ceremonial dances —
your joyful daybreak
twirls and swirls
when confronted
with gold and orange hues
muddled with a soporific
daub of soft lavender,
greeting playfully
every crevice of the land;
tell me, my friend,
how long can bear cubs
cling to their precious lives
without a mother,
without her nurturing
warm embrace

and milk to sustain
their growing appetite?

How, then, do you expect
to sever your relationship
with the fountainhead,
to which you owe
your every molecule?

Trust in what birthed you.
Not in your selfish reveries.

CATCHING YOUR EYE
Lowen Puckey

Your looks won't work here.

Sky stripped of studded references, two eyes meeting in eternal
night.
Announce your intent: *I am an unfolding perpetuem.*

Do not blindside me. I see, in my own ways, exactly as is.
Let me hear your voice, telling me who you are.
Don't assume you know what I need.
Do not excuse me, sight unseen.

All is in my hands. *Look: trace my ways.*

Come closer — you must come closer to know what I have
become.
Not all are made in the same mould; not all lives are lived to the
same end.
The soul needs to see, hand upon hand, touching the Grande Art
withheld,
experiencing beyond two dimensional impossibilities.

Here is touch

Here is sound

Here is heat eternal

See what you like. You may not see through me
- I know
that you are there:

ask me. Just ask me.
I, also,
am here.

REVELATION
Jenny N. Olson

I am a creature of the earth, mischievous and lithe, roaming
through the forest.
Savage branches rip the light fabric of my dress.

Barefoot, my perennially pointed ballerina toes dance,
caressing a pool of soft mud which pleads with me to paint my
body.

Mesmerized, I let my hands knead deep into the earth's clay as my
dress is discarded.

My canvas, a blending of curved flesh welcomes
the stroke as my mud covered body becomes
dressed in artistic desires.

Light streaming between the trees catches my eye and invites me
to play.
Shadows come alive, showering me with fluttering specks of
sunlight that beckon me like a spotlight.

I begin to dance…

I am graceful, strong, and *achingly alive,*
as my entire being is overcome with revelation.
A dancer's superpower is to speak without words.

Elation, rage, jealousy, doubt and triumph pour from me like the
voyage of a cascading waterfall.

As I dance even the harshest emotions cannot control me,
for we have become partners of expression.
All feelings, essential steps that connect our choreography.
*The absence of just one, and the complete human experience fails
to exist.*

I long to exist so deeply, and for these moments as I dance, that is
exactly what I do.

The sky clouds over, the curtain has come down on my dance.

Words are overrated.
I may never speak again.

COLLISION SCENE
Heath Houston

He bumped into her because he was checking, for the fourth time, that he had his keys, wallet, and phone in his pockets. One, two, three, all there, confirmed in a two handed maneuver reminiscent of spectacles, testicles, wallet, and watch. He seemed incapable of doing this without looking down in concentration. He made a quick nod to himself as his hand passed at last over the shape of the phone in his pocket.

She bumped into him because she was certain there was something in her shoe. She knew she should have worn flats. At least with those a quick kick and wiggle would confirm the existence or absence of a foreign object without the chance of flinging a pump into an unsuspecting pedestrian's face. Coffee in one hand, phone in the other, she looked down as if the furrowing of her brow would shame the shoe into confessing.

He looked up at the moment of impact, her eyes hazel, her mouth partially open in surprise; these things registered as the sides her coffee cup collapsed, sending the plastic lid towards her and the dark liquid arcing gracefully over and onto his shoulder. Hot droplets struck his ear and neck but mostly his jacket, his left eye closing in automatic response. Her phone seemed to hover mid-air after leaving her hand.

She looked up at the moment of impact, his one eye blue, the other closed, mouth making the oddest contortion as her coffee leapt from the compressed cup, the green lid gracefully ejected towards her forehead. The phone slipped from her hand as she collided. The coffee looked like a sheet of molten brown glass draping his shoulder before it struck the jacket. She gasped involuntarily.

His right arm went around her as she pushed into him, her mouth still in an O of surprise, both of her empty hands between them now. The coffee cup had passed his field of vision, tumbling chaotically over his shoulder. The green lid bounced off her forehead, leaving a few drops of coffee above her left eyebrow. He could feel the warm liquid begin to soak his shirt. He had instinctively reached for the airborne phone with his other hand, managing only to swat it, sending it back at her.

Her hands grasped the fabric of his shirt and jacket to steady herself as she felt his arm support her from behind. He was grinning now which only confused her more. The lid of her coffee cup struck her in the forehead; she could feel a droplet on her eye lashes, the cup itself flying over his shoulder and into the window of a passing car. She heard the squeal of tires, but her attention was more on the way he inexplicably konged her phone like it was a volleyball, sending it past her left ear.

His eyes followed the phone as it just skimmed her hair and continued past her to strike a man, in an expensive looking suit, in the bridge of his nose. In seeming slow motion, the man's arm lifted in belated defense, the briefcase in that hand breaking free. At the same time he heard the squeal of tires as a car swerved out of control. He felt her weight on his arm and the grip of her hands on his shirt. She was pretty, he thought, as she tugged on him.

"Shit!" she heard, loudly, from behind her. In her peripheral vision she noticed a briefcase flying through the air, coming from the same direction. She was pressed into him now, looking up. He was handsome, she thought, as she let his arm steady her. She winced at the sound of a loud crash, also behind her, down the street. There was a large police patrolman walking briskly in their direction, concerned eyes focused intently past them.

He felt her hands release the fabric of his shirt as she got her feet properly under her, feeling a sudden small pang of regret that he'd need to remove his arm from her at some point. He smelled a lovely scent on her, just barely detected over the smell of his coffee soaked jacket. The man in the suit was going down onto the sidewalk. She really was lovely looking up at him. Down the street a car swerved into oncoming traffic causing one… two… three cars to crash so far… Ooo, make that four, he thought with a wince. One of those car doors had opened and a man was running away from it towards them.

She relaxed her hands now, palms pressed flat between them. She found his smile curious as he looked down at her with both lovely blue eyes and she felt her mouth start to turn up at the corners in response. The briefcase had just struck the patrolman in the head, knocking him flat and releasing a flurry of papers and white dust billowing into the air. She heard shouts from behind her, following several loud crashes. She found herself appreciating the feel of his arm around her.

He found it difficult to focus on anything else but her at the moment, barely registering a large tanker truck coming onto the street, near the crashes, faster than it should be. The man in the suit was on his feet, dusting himself off and looking around, a panicked expression on his face. He noticed a tiny smile beginning to form on her lips. It made her even prettier. Several more people were now running in their direction from the crashes. There was definitely something on fire over there. He could make out fetching little freckles on her face.

She noticed there was no ring on his left hand, which was resting gently on her upper arm. The patrolman was sitting up now, looking confused, face plastered with white powder, surrounded with papers, some of them fluttering around in the

the breeze. She pressed even closer to him as a giant explosion erupted from down the street behind her. A few people were running past them on either side. His hand tightening slightly on her arm. She had really soaked him with coffee, she thought, as she automatically pressed her face against his shoulder in response to the explosion.

His eyes went wide as the tanker plowed into the crashed cars, the driver jumped out and scrambled, barely clearing the fireball that erupted. The driver was hot on the heels of the running crowd, most of whom were headed towards him and the hazel-eyed lady. He felt her face press against him, the breeze causing her hair to tickle his nose. He breathed deeply enjoying how she smelled. The man in the suit was running ahead of the pack like Jesse Owens, passing them along with a few others.

She pulled her head back, feeling a little dizzy, whether from his eyes, the impact, his arms, or the explosion. Over his shoulder she saw a man in an expensive suit running like dogs were after him. The patrolman was on his feet and looking pissed off, nightstick in hand, face still powdered like a particularly unpleasant-looking kabuki actor. She felt a heat from behind her as well as a heat in her face as she realized her palms were pressed against his chest.

He looked back down at her again as she lifted her head. There was an attractive flush to her face that he hadn't noticed before. The charging crowd split around them as if Moses had commanded it. He barely noticed it but for the wind, sound, and the occasional piece of clothing brushing his arm. He was conscious now of his hand against her back and could feel a quickening to her breathing. It made him smile even more.

She lifted her eyes to meet his. Seeing his smile prompted her to make one of her own. The patrolman reeled his arm back with the nightstick as the man in the suit neared him. She and the blue-eyed man were surrounded on all sides now by a crowd running at full speed. He moved his hand from her arm to join the other at her back. The patrolman swung the stick, taking the man in the suit completely off his feet before the crowd engulfed them both.

"Hi," he said, still holding her, still smiling, blue eyes possibly twinkling.

"Hello," she said, returning a somewhat coy, but no less genuine, smile, her own eyes threatening a twinkle as well.

SILVER
Noha Medhat

You kill every conversation
With the edge
Of your sword.

Your blades are razor
Blade~sharp
And wildly sore.

I sit there
And feel
Like a stabbed princess
In blood.

A mud
Of dark silence
And unwavering pain
Descend upon me.

And I'm stuck
To think twice
And question the sword.

Does it want to kill me
Or just break
My core?

SEVENTEEN
Lisa Sellge

My sister's innocence
has left on the 6pm train,
has taken leave of her body
has gone to bring the boys home.

My sister's innocence
fell down the stairs
drank purple champagne
took a free ride.

My sister's innocence
laid down laughing
laid down dancing
laid down the law.

My sister's innocence
was stripped in flight
was tricked and treated
was passed under the table.
My sister is innocent.

DESIRING TO SEE THE PLEIADES
Zev Akhter

A shoot-up of foxgloves –

hummingbirds   with their
longer-than-body, larger-than-life, beaks
I have seen drink from

            the holy ambrosia.

& when under the Taurean moonlight
they sway in the wind,

crystallized amethyst   apatite,
tinkle for a moment like Parisian bells.

You, born under the sign of Aphrodite,
why must your own beauty not transcend;

    & why not your mind aesthetic.

*He will not be handled by human hand,
not in this given life,* Lucie's line,
but apt too, to our bull.

May the mariposan bull keep seeing
the depth of beauty in everything,
till eternity.

I levy upon your ever sacrosanct soul,

    your eyes, a league of powerful

            bards, born under this sun.

PHASES, SEASON CHANGES
Rachel B. Baxter

He is, as every man is,
A son of earthly history.
And she is as every daughter —
A crescent moon,
A smile on its side.
She is essential to everything else,
Though suspended in the dark canopy.
Soon they'll take their sides,
His Earth and her Tides,
Agreeing to disagree.

Her first memory is far away,
It's as far as eyes reach down the road,
It sleeps not soundly on the sea floor.
Do you remember when winter
Began in December and
Not a day before?

But, here, weather patterns turn like
A virgin mind on cheap wine —
Lying on her side,
She smiled reflecting the
Feeble (but present!) glow of
That pale, pale sun.

His face is shown, but his heat is
Too weak to blanket the Earth —
She has a feeling that this

Is concerning something
She has slept through,
Maybe a lecture on orbits,
Gravitations, and the change in seasons.
Though, to her, these explanations had no use —
If it is change you want to see,
Just look at me…
And he did, often.
An eclipse was never rare.

So, January descends
And in his hands he
Gently cradles a face
So full now and cold from
The winter's chilling bite,
It's such a nice night
She may say in an alluring way~
I know, stumbling on words,
It's amazing,
I was just about to say…

INTO THE ABYSS

Burying the ashes of the Leviathan
Leah J.

into depths, I bury
the ashes of the Leviathan

burnt roots and gnarled trees
once the soul's compass

banish to the abyss, this primordial shadow
go without, to the wilderness, butterfly

with a low, dawning sun
the mist recedes, after torrent of rains

illuminating sculptures, beneath
as doves flock, with lofty clouds

diamonds see clearly, the burning gold
awash, in that vast cerulean sea

SARCOMA
Theo Beecroft

My heart beats as I shake off the dread. I can feel my bare ass on the linoleum cover of the bench as I play with the edge of the green robes between my coarse fingers. How many times have I sat in these waiting rooms just before a fight? I try to count but I run out of fingers and toes. There were those small regional matches back when I was kid, barely worth a thought now, and then the ones when I hit my twenties, the ones where a man really gets his mettle, tests himself against the rest of the world. I was all blood and muscle back then, all spit and sweat in the ring, so fast that a guy didn't realise I'd hit him until he was laid on the canvas. My body did most of the work those days, only a little technique but it was enough with the nerves I had, the heart and the lungs that wouldn't even consider stopping.

You get to thinking that there isn't a single man alive that can bring you down until you meet the veterans from the upper circuits. You're all flash and pubescent anger but they've had time, almost millennia, to hone themselves a fine needle point. I came out swinging against John "The Bronze" Geel in 91' and he dropped me before the first bell with the kind of haymaker that tells you just how many guys hadn't gotten back up after it'd connected. I rose to my feet that night because it's that or nothing, and by the fifth, I'd worked a counter game that scraped me through to win on points. You think that you've overcome a hurdle, as though you've managed to survive something that could have killed you, so you must be stronger for it, but then you fight more of these guys and every one's different. Simone "the Salmon" Ellis, a southpaw much faster than me that had me on the ropes right up until the twelfth when he started to flag and I could put him away; Avi Cena, a Greek, raw~muscle kind of fighter who took huge shots at my head and who I had to overpower early on before he could get a good rhythm going; Burrill Crohn, a wiry little thing that danced around me taking pot~shots at my midsection for seven rounds until I threw a lucky straight that sent him off balance and managed to knock him out by the ninth. You can prepare as much as you like, and it helps, but these guys, so precise and always so silent in the ring, it's as much chance as it is skill that keeps you going against them.

I inject. The chances of winning are practically nil without a chemical edge. Illegality doesn't even factor into it, you take everything you can get, or you lose. The spectators rumble and cry outside in uneven waves, like a choppy sea beyond the up~swerve of a rising cliff.

Time to go.

Hector Lionel Foma, also known by his sobriquet "The Crab" on account of the size of his fists in proportion to his arms. I had been in the ring with Foma before, back when he'd first come into the circuit, and it was, without a doubt, the hardest fight of my life. He was sloppy back then, but you just could not get the man to go down. I landed a right cross in the twelfth that finished things, I'd thought for good, with a cut so deep you might call it more of an incision. TKO, I heard a man in white say beneath the ringing in my ears. I saw Foma sat in the corner like a piece of meat, all bloodied and swelling with each breath, his eyes clear and staring back into mine. No handshakes after that. Not many normal fighters get back to anything after what I'd done to him, but Foma isn't exactly what you'd call a normal fighter.

A year later, I heard that he beat a friend of mine from the tenements back home, the kind of kid that had a lot of reasons to want to get into a ring with just about anybody but not a bad guy. I couldn't recognise him in the photos afterwards. Then I started hearing about a lot of guys losing to Foma, how he had this knack for taking out experienced boxers, no matter how many wins, no matter how many knock outs, he just didn't stop, and they couldn't take him. Their faces cross through my mind as I walk to the ring.

Wrong thoughts. Clarity now.

The crowd roars like a single animal as I walk through the stadium, the cry goes up into the air and hangs there in the dark. I can't see any faces, just the shadows writhing. The ring has that sterile look, fluorescent in an off way that never seemed to fit, and Bergman puts his hand on my shoulder. Bergman, my coach, has this forthright face, somehow not even practiced, it's just how it rests. The man knows every angle of a fight, as much as can be seen from a corner, at least. He's seen every punch thrown by Foma over his career, every shift of weight and bloody knockout. His words are correct in that earnest simplicity which almost makes you doubt him, they're so clear. He's never lied to me; never given me an ounce of insincerity and I hope that he knows just how much that means. We both understand that the prognosis is doubtful on this one, but he's cut from the same cloth as me and I haven't walked away from a fight yet. We've worked on a long game plan for this thing, endure whatever Foma can throw at me and outlast him, grind him down with body shots until he shrinks into a corner exhausted, it's the only chance that I've got in there with him.

I look across the canvas and I see him for the first time in five years under strange green lights that blow through me but define him clearly against the dark. He's like a lump of gristle, close to bursting with muscle and purpose. There's no one with him, he just enters in silence and sits placidly across from me. Half a decade and he's used the time damn well, where once he even stood unsure, he's now got that assured sense of self. He is exactly where he wants to be. There's always something off about Foma, a sort of unpredictability that doesn't fit with how static he is out of the ring. His face has a way of contorting so quickly that you barely register it. He looks like some imposter, a parody of the human form made autonomous.

Still the heart. Breathe slow.

The announcer quiets the crowd, I didn't know that they could be silenced at all, but he manages it with just the raise of a hand. Some of these guys have that showman flash but this one's almost deadpan, direct in introduction. After Foma's name, the dark rumbles with the deep bass hum that courses through me. After mine, I hear a few clear voices cut across the surging crowd, the voices that matter because I recognise them: Mona's falsetto, my father's baritone, my son's teenage voice breaking. They clear out the rest.

The referee calls for a clean fight, but everyone here knows that isn't how this is going down. Foma doesn't fight fair and I don't intend to let him have his way. The man just stares at me blankly as we touch gloves, he's so alive I can feel his pulse in rhythm with my own. The bell rings out with the crowd and we begin this damnable thing.

I get a feel for the man as I throw out a few jabs. You learn more about your opponent in these first rounds than their loved ones do in a lifetime: the cut of their mind, their history of violence in the ring. Foma's faster than I remember and insidious in the way he draws you into a false sense of security. He lets me get in a few big shots, leaving his body open and feeling the strength that I have behind each punch, he's measuring me here, trying to see what I can do to him, but I've got the sense to hold back a little, always watching for any openings I might leave myself.

He throws some real steam rollers, huge punches with obvious wind ups that'd floor me if they connected but I know how to weave, I swerve out from under him more times than I can count and nothing of his seems to stick until the end of the third when he changes up his game a little with this one-two cross that catches me off guard.

The bell rings and he stops, mid hook, barely dejected as he trundles off back to his corner. I swill the water and I can taste iron in my mouth. Spit it out. Breathe in deep. Keep breathing, it's what Bergman always tells me. He knows how this works, he's seen the way Foma fights and he tells me not to let up, don't get complacent at all because this guy can floor me in a second if I give him an opening. Somehow, Mona's ringside and she squeezes my arm. It kills her to see me out here, I can see it on her face, but she gives me that smile that fills me up inside. I glance across at

Foma. He still doesn't have anyone in his corner. He just stares back at me without emotion and suddenly I feel almost embarrassed to need so many people around me. His chest doesn't heave, and he looks smaller out there on the other side of the square. I must look just as small. The bell rings again, and I get to my feet.

Foma's changed up again, this is one of the key parts of his game — his unpredictability. I'm having to feel him out every round out here because any openings he gives me are snares, setups for some punishing counter that I only just manage to block. I get to the sixth and I can feel my lungs burning as I circle around him. He's solid, almost stock still from the waist down, and I'm having to draw the punches out of him. Then, all at once, he throws a slow straight to my temple that I counter, and he clutches up close and rams his forehead into my face. Blood spurts and my eyes scrunch up with the phosphorescent pain. He pushes me back to the ropes and it's all I can do to hold up my arms as he ploughs uppercuts into my abdomen. The referee pulls him off eventually. The seconds tick by, they're all that I can think about whilst he works me over, and I'm ragged by the time I make it back to my corner.

He's managed to get to my liver, I can feel him pumping through my veins. Bergman tells me to breathe, it's harder and harder to take that advice. His face is stone still and serious as he tells me what's happening in there. On the other side of the ring, I see Foma sitting calmly. He's breathing, I can tell, but not as hard as I am. There's this strange way that he seems to change — he sort of swells in small increments until he's almost unrecognisable after a few rounds. Somehow the notion that he looks quite a bit like me has gotten into my head and it rings there, purposefully. A game plan has to be fluid, you have to adapt to an opponent or you'll fight how he wants you to. Bergman sees how bad this sort of thing gets once it's taken a hold and tells me to get aggressive, shock and awe, "Blitzkreig" is the word he uses. Put the man down. He has to tell me to get back in, I barely hear the bell over the crash of the crowd.

I am invasive, I am direct. His punches connect and so do

mine. It is bloody and ugly and the seconds swim by us through the viscera. A human body, even an older one like mine, has a natural instinct to survive. Basal, I feel it throb at the top of my spine. Every muscle contracts and pushes into the correct angle. It's mathematical, surgical, beautiful even, if not for the mess that my gloves are connecting with. He falters, staggers after I land an errant left hook that catches him off guard, and I bring my fist down like a hammer against his fleshy jaw. He hits the canvas with a thud that ripples up through my legs. I am in disbelief and I can't take my swollen eyes off of him: suddenly diminutive in a way that I didn't think possible. The referee gets to the count of seven before the bell rings and I feel just how much that took out of me when I fall back into my corner.

Perhaps, for the first time in my life, I see Bergman smile at me. It's pained somehow but I give him one back. There's a small cut on my forehead which he diligently covers in vaseline. My hair comes out with wipes of the towel. I hear the croak of my son in the crowd, I think of him on the cusp of his life and I wish that he couldn't see this. My father is quiet, but I hear his breathing, cracked in a way I haven't noticed before. I am amazed that I can hear him above everyone else. Mona is silent, and tears run down her still face. It costs them so much for me to be here. It is a sad thing to look back up at the man across from me. Foma has an incredible tenacity. He remains calm with the blood running down his face. His eyes don't break from mine and he breathes deep.

When we get back into the ring together, there's something strange in his eyes as he regards me, a sort of contemplation which I didn't think him capable of, a malignant intelligence. I had thought to use my momentum but I'm flagging as much as he is and it's hard going. We trade blows and clutch together like one and the same animal, but I feel a shift in him, a second wind beyond human endurance that I didn't know he was capable of. The round ends, and I have lost something.

When I get back in there with him, he's woken up in some way. My arms come at him weaker than before and he moves around me with a dizzying combination of blows that throw me off balance. I feel off centre, and when his fist crashes into my nose like a 12 gauge blast my legs give out and I spin to the floor in a cascade of lens flashes. I feel as though there is cotton in my ears. My innards roil, and my lungs fail. Foma stands a ways off as I am transfixed by how much blood is streaming from my mouth. It splays like some sanguine flower. I hear the referee shout out a "five" and then Mona's voice, quiet but with me, just saying "please". I am up by the 9 but I am no longer myself, I feel something wrong in the pit of my stomach. My head sings out of tune and its pieces don't fit together any more.

I have never felt so alone. Now, between rounds, Bergman's advice is drowned out by a low hum. I can't see my family any more, I don't look into the crowd even though I know that they just want to help me somehow. I am ashamed and alone. Foma looms faceless now, a bubbling mass of rippling tissue in the ring. My cross counter doesn't cut it, not against that mindless thing. It swells, bursts and spills over the trembling canvas, and you see how small a man is next to something so insane, aimless, and deadly. He grows and spreads until he is the ring itself and I am surrounded by him. He is in every pore of my body, abhorrent and deep in every cell. My legs barely hold me upright and I cannot remember life before getting into this ring. I reach the end of the fourteenth round and I am broken in more ways than I can count. I run out of fingers and toes.

I never thought that I would choose to quit. I will lose this fight, it's not even a potential now, just an inevitability, and I get to thinking about how much another three minutes in there is going to be worth.

Doctor Bergman tells me to keep breathing, he was always one of the best, but I see that towel, pink and splotched with my blood. I see that thing still growing in there, unstoppable and blind. I am afraid. Afraid of what it'll do to me before I lose. I can't bear for anyone else to see but, more than that, more than anything, I can't bear to see myself pulled down to the floor before I go, withered and skeletal before that abomination, as it grinds me into a pulpy mess of a man. That's not how I want to go out. I take off my gloves and feel the cotton of the towel between my coarse fingers. I feel the texture and it's all that I've ever felt. I am so sorry to those that loved me. The fabric falls into the ring and I step out of that square of light, out into the screaming dark.

THERE IS LIFE IN THE SILENCE
Giulia de Gregorio Listo

Turned inside out
I've been screaming
But, perhaps, in a different language.
One nobody knows nor cares to understand.

Feels like I've been scratching the inside of a cave
But the cave is me, bleeding from the upper side of my torso
To the thinnest part of my ankles,
Where bones and tendons agglomerate into intense pain,
Twisting the soul, squeezing from it the sounds,
The shrieks of extinct animals and lost ancestors.
It is not the pain that is new or puzzling to me, though,
But the inability to end it.

It is the bluntness of my teeth, unable to bite off
The parts that ache.
It is the acidity of my tongue, unable to lick it clean,
Only burning the skin, dissolving it into a mixture
Of incapacity and fear, and all of the things that
Stop one by the knees, that bend them down into a prayer,
A chant of despair.

When I look into the mirror, a black hole seems to stare back.
It is not emptiness nor dullness.
It is craving, consuming more and more and more
But expelling nothing.
Perhaps a word or two, misspelt, weak, low, not making sense.
The crackle from the streets is a more pleasing sound

Than what comes out of my inhospitable astronomical mouth.

I remember waking up from a dream where I was talking to
Jupiter.
Its grandeur accepted to sit down for a warm tea, and we chatted.
We went on about life's unfairness and why, of all things,
I proclaimed myself a poet.
A harvester of humans' innermost sorrows.
A dictionary of all that is somehow interlaced between
The mundane daily life and the oppressive burning of the cosmos.
Jupiter had no answers but silence. The silence that had
surrounded me.
The silence of the dark hole in the mirror.
The silence of the pain crossing my body as a belated train,
Apologizing yet not slowing down for a second.

There is life in the silence.

That was the phrase I woke up to.
That was the answer.
Creation was not only chaos and turbulence and explosions.
It could be the muffled sound of a hand against a sheet of paper,
Which exists but loses itself amidst the noise of civilization.
Yet it creates. It endures. It generates.

It could be the quiet hurt of not knowing what to say
Properly
For weeks
Until the poem is ready
Loud
And screamed into the world.

So maybe I've been saying the right things,
Creating the right way,
Only silently inside my head
Where black holes dissolve into life,
And I haunt back, out loud, the words that haunt me.

DISCO LIGHTS ON STEROIDS
Yedu Bose

Her palms moved gracefully away from her body
They formed spirals and waded through the air
"Dude, I'm partying the fuck out of tomorrow"
There was happiness etched on her face
Like a wind chime that's aware of an imminent gust

I looked her in the eyes and smiled for her bliss
This obnoxious spendthrift of smiles and winks
A blistering rainbow celebrating its sentient glory
Putting out the fires in her life
With a pair of dancing shoes
And a look of kindness anyone is free to steal off her face

A mumble and a nod
I am staring at my own life once again
And all I see are spectacles and cowardice
The latter always the incentive of the former
Depression is often like a cartwheeling child
Dirty fingered and stupid enough to enjoy inverting its own world

Are there parties out there I could belong in?
A safe space I could convince myself it was okay to let go
I grin at myself and imagine letting go
Blaring house music and tattered inhibitions
Swirling bodies and angry self detachment
A coterie of contentment
Shimmering elusive and cruel
Among disco lights allegedly on steroids

WHERE HOPE LIVES

Stella J. McKenna

Hope lives in the pink sunsets,
on the ocean waves,
in the snow-dusted crocus stems.

It's in the whole avocado,
the freshly-baked, cooling pie,
the fun-sized pack of Starbursts.

Hope hides in the unopened envelope,
the email,
the text message.
Rarely, the phone call.

It's when you dip your foot in the water,
turn the corner from a headwind,
scan the aisle for parking spots.

It's while you wait for your luggage,
shake the dice in your hands,
search the rack for your size.

Sometimes it's in a whisper,
a wink,
a secretive smile,
a playful nudge.

Hope lingers in the moment before your lips touch,
and the moments after, too.

It's when you hop on the end of a queue,
after you place your order,
uncork a new bottle.

Hope lies inside the new thing,
but also in the broken thing.

I found hope in his eyes once,
and it spilled into mine.
The most beautiful hope, I remember.
Not even the pink sunsets compare.

SHOULD THE HANDS OF TIME TICK BACKWARDS
Valentine Nnebe

Should the hands of time tick backwards
to meet an infant nursed on tender breasts
wriggling, set in a crib, pampered to rest.
Who soaks the atmosphere with joy
more so being found a boy.

Should the hands of time tick backwards
to a child kit in uniforms and socks
strapped with a bag and snacks in a box,
crying at dad's goodbyes
battling separation
so harsh you thought he would die.

Should the hands of time tick backwards
when young girls and pretty teens were the fancy —
slender, garish in skinny jeans.
When looks and carriage were thought to matter more,
they became a habit, *a weakness with a flaw.*

Should the hands of time tick backwards
to make me appease all my bruised souls
and align my derailed goals.

To cherish the light seen in people's eyes,
wiping the saline tears of their cries.
Knowing their ghost for a whiff of smoke,
could depart untimely from this earthly yoke.

May the hands of time tick backwards
then my toxic acts will I first arrest,
adopting the heart of an angel for my guest.
This will keep my soul at rest
assured to have ordered my very life's best.

DANCING FOR PEACE
Crystal Jackson

They say dance as if no one's looking.

Dance as if you'll die tomorrow.

Just dance.

But I say: No.

Dance as if this moment in time is all that will ever be.

> Dance as if your feet were kissing the floor
> And your fingertips were stroking the sky.

Dance as if your words were starlight
And your hands moving through the air made flowers bloom.

Dance as if your hips moving to the beat pulled in the tide
And your labored breath brought every child that will be into the world.

> Dance as if the rhythm of your movements
> Sent the world spinning and gave birth to
> galaxies.

Dance as if your sweat fed rivers that wore paths through tall mountains,

As if your aching legs could absorb the heartache of the world.

Dance as if dancing brought an end to tyrants,
As if a war of movement could usher in peace.

Dance until you are exhausted and elated,
Until your fury and sadness are spent.

Dance until all that is left Is the ecstasy of the dance.

FALLEN APPLE
Remington Write

Being the daughter of a famous suicide is a valid career path. One bullet and no door has ever been closed to me.

On the last Tuesday of October in 1962, a jewel of a day with the kind of blue sky that makes you want to cry, my mother put her notebooks in order, chronologically, and sent a final draft of her last poetry collection to her agent. My sister and I were at our babysitter's so the only one to hear the report of the pistol was our old dog, Grunt.

Can I write?

I can, but it doesn't matter all that much. A powerhouse agency swooped in and poached me away from Mother's perplexed agent, Uncle Bobby, the minute my second novel was optioned. Uncle Bobby knew when he was beaten and, besides, Mother had taken care of him in her meticulous will. He wished me well and retired to Costa Rica.

My sister went for the cliché of drugs and alcohol.

Her messy memoir is not selling. The market is saturated, true, but it's just badly written. She's still pissed that I declined to add a blurb to the jacket. I hope she's getting to those meetings as I'd prefer she not drink herself to death but I also prefer not to be associated with crap.

I've got this book tour coming up. My second ex, the lazy

s.o.b., won alimony in the divorce and I'm writing checks while my assistant packs. Pissed or not, my sister always cashes the monthly check I send. Mother may have hated her fame but she was happy enough to spread the money around and it's been up to me to bring money back to the fame. I snap the checkbook shut and reach for my glass of chilled green tea.

"Excuse me, Miss Seagal, which laptop do you want to take?"

"What? Oh, I don't know, the smallest one, the lightest." Gianna is thorough but annoying and I'd appreciate more initiative on her part.

I pick up the itinerary again; Christ, why does that bastard Dilkin insist on a dartboard approach to booking? Chicago, Atlanta, Portland (Maine), Kansas City (Kansas), Santa Fe, Miami, Boise (Boise?), Dallas, Minneapolis, San Diego, Pittsburgh, Los Angeles and then, finally, New York. When did book tours become a form of punishment? I used to love being the rockstar, didn't I?

"Excuse me, Miss Seagal, should I pack your fur?"

"What do *you* think, Gianna? It's fucking September. Use your brain for something besides separating your ears." She forgets that she's standing behind me facing the mirror and I get the full blast of her silent fury for the second it takes for her to compose herself. I thought this one would work out, but I'm having my doubts. Nothing for it now. It's too late to break in a new one.

And the telephone rings. It's Dilkin. Let him talk to voice mail. Jesus, but he loves the sound of his own voice. I motion for Gianna to hand me my hairbrush, aiming my flashiest smile into the mirror. She smiles back and hands it to me. I shouldn't, but cannot resist one tiny poke.

"Thanks, G. Call Anton, you need a trim and a threading before we go." I touch my forefinger to the point between my own nicely separated eyebrows and wink.

The phone rings again. Jesus. I don't even look at it, just hand it to Gianna. She's not smiling now. I go back to brushing my hair, not really paying attention until the phone is suddenly thrust at me. Gianna's face is tight.

"It's Mr. Dilkin. Won't take no for an answer."

"Now what?" If nothing else, I can take someone else's head off this morning. Dilkin's grows back pretty quickly.

"Mindy's disappeared. She left a letter."

"What do you mean 'disappeared'? She's always off with some new man. She'll be around to cash her check."

"No, you need to read this letter. She's about to pull some stunt."

"Read it to me."

"Nope, not me. I'm bringing it over." *Click.* Drama queen. And just to heighten the soap opera, he texts: *we may have to ditch tour.*

That suits me, but my publisher isn't going to ditch this tour. Dilkin's gone off his meds or he's been reading my mother's poetry again. Can I add the caveat to my next contract for a publicist that they must have never heard of my mother? It's not so unlikely. After all, it's not as if she was Sylvia fucking Plath for christ's sake.

"Hide the vodka and put out something to eat. Dilkin's on his way over."

I have read Mindy's letter three times and it's crazier with each reading. But she's not crazy and I need to come up with a plan. Fast. I'm due in Chicago tomorrow evening. Clearly, I've been underestimating my drug-addled little sister for some time now.

This really verges on genius.

"Ok, here's what we're going to do." Gianna and Dilkin actually lean forward. This is the best I have to bring to this little war? I may be in real trouble here. "G., you leave right now and prepare the staff in Chicago. Don't tell them too much, just make sure they know what may happen and what to ignore." She sits there, all expectant and confused. "Go! Now! Go on, you know who to call at the airlines. I want you in Chicago in three hours. Get them ready."

She hussles out and I turn to Dilkin. "You get to Atlanta and do the same. Get going. You know how to handle this."

"We can't leapfrog through the whole tour like this. She'll have already talked to the people in Sante Fe and Boise before we even hit Chicago."

"No, she won't." I know who I have to call now. "She's got to be sure we're playing our part in this before she can approach each next location." I pause, then grab a piece of paper and pen. "Here, get this press release out."

They're gone and now I look at my phone like it's rotted. I have to dial the number because I dumped it from the phone's memory years ago. I doubt I'll ever dump it from my memory, dammit. Two rings, what am I going to say if it goes to voice mail? Oh, let it go to voice mail. I'll think of something.

"That took longer than I thought it would." His voice still does that thing to me.

"Go ahead. Gloat. It gets better: I need your help." I wait.

"Why would I help you?"

"Old time's sake?"

"Not good enough." He's smiling. I can hear it.

"Because your ex-wife is about to wreck my life and my career."

"You'll recall why she's my ex, yes?"

"Don't even. This is a conversation you do not want to start."

"Sure I do. It'll relieve the boredom."

"You're the one who checked yourself into that place, don't whine now if it's not to your liking." I need to watch it, I really do need Ty's help, but Jesus, he gets under my skin.

"This is fun. What kind of mess has my little Mindy unleashed this time?"

"She sent a letter to my publicist and says she's going to commit suicide at one of my readings on this book tour."

"You can't believe she's serious. The woman is so much of a wreck that she still hasn't signed off on the divorce." He goes quiet and I wait. "Since when have you gotten so easily spooked?"

"You didn't read the letter."

"Bring it to me." It's not a request.

"I don't have time. I have to be in Chicago tomorrow. Look, just call her. Talk to her."

"Oh, you are delusional, cupcake. I can't think of a surer way to have her dangling in front of the Barnes & Noble at State and Elm."

"You're wrong. I seduced you, remember?" Call me cupcake?

"I'll need to read the letter if I'm going to be of any use in this farce."

"I'll courier a copy."

I can feel it happening; those old sticky tendrils of hope. "Thanks." *Click.* Quick. Am I safe? No, and I never have been around this man. Not from the moment Mindy brought him to my first book release. I shake my head, like I can dislodge something stuck, and arrange a copy of this time bomb delivered to the man who may very well turn out to be the fuse.

I was so impressed with everything back then, including myself.

Especially myself.

That book release was like Christmas morning, the first warm day of spring and falling in love all at the same time. The night before, I couldn't close my eyes and was still riding my adrenaline high through the day and into the next night. I wore my first ever couture outfit and when I walked into that room, I owned it.

The fact that half the luminaries in the room were there looking for a fault line, a soft place to pry open and poke around in, only increased my sense of power. They were looking for signs of suicide and I gave them a collective bitch slap. The novel has been proclaimed dead for decades, so it always surprises everyone when another novel takes off.

Mine was rocketing out of the stratosphere.

Moving with ease from circle to circle, I made my rounds of the room, sipping one glass of prosecco. Of course I'd had to invite Mindy but had decided that any boneheaded crap she might pull could not touch me. If the vultures wanted a good look at their future suicide Mindy would certainly provide it.

So, when she arrived, I was ready to welcome her with genuine ease. I heard her before I saw her, poor kid totally inherited Father's ghastly titter when she was nervous. I was happy to finish with a certain powerful agent, leaving her to wonder if she'd hooked me or not, and turned to greet my sister.

The worst writers call it a lightning bolt, the better ones will toss a grenade in the general direction, but the best writers aim for that perfect throat shot before squeezing off their round. Every hackneyed cliché crackled and fell when the man standing next to Mindy looked at me. Christ, he wasn't even all that, really. Ty isn't tall, he's not really great looking and he's losing his hair. But what he's got he knows how to use and when he looked at me he took me.

Mindy, being mildly toasted, noticed nothing. She was tricked out in some ridiculous stab at bohemian-cool and launched into her steady stream of consciousness the moment I got in earshot. I reminded myself that she couldn't touch me tonight as heads turned, bent and whispered. Even so, I steered the two of them away from the drinks table.

"Nice turnout." Ty inserted.

"Oh, right! Sorry, sorry," and away she went, winding through an overlong introduction that began with where Ty's parents honeymooned and how he was conceived.

I was not then, and am still not, easily duped.

The warning sirens were blasting and I was sort of paying attention to them. He was trouble. I hadn't had enough trouble at that point to understand why the sirens were so loud. Trouble, in my still soft comprehension, was merely another source of material. My compromise was to go off with him for a second glass of wine, let his arm graze mine and then shuck him off for that still circling agent.

He didn't call or email or make one move in my direction. I stood by an open door, waiting for nothing. I got to work on the next book. The first one got optioned for a movie with some real names signing on to push it to its second life. Time did not do what it's supposed to do and, at least once a day, I checked for something that was not there.

If time wasn't going to do it, I had to take drastic action: I got married.

"She was bluffing all along." Dilkin was on his third scotch after the signing in Pittsburgh.

I hold out my glass. Gianna quit back in Boise, so it's been Dilkin and I slogging across the country like some inane snake oil show. The readers, bless their bored, pointless little hearts, have been lining up. The publisher will be happy although my editor's already been on my ass about the next book.

"We're not home free yet, champ. Don't go and fucking jinx us."

"Oh, come on, you knew she was just messing with your head." He drains the glass and makes to reach for the bottle.

"Enough." I sweep the bottle out of his reach, topping off my own glass. "We still got LA and then New York to get through and, think about this, where would she make a bigger splash than by offing herself there?"

"I can't believe you give her that much space in your head. You know what a ditz she is! Give me that bottle. Just one more." He makes a grab for the bottle, but Dilkin never could hold his liquor and I easily keep it out of reach.

"Go to bed and don't even think of whining about a hangover tomorrow. We're up at eight, no matter what. Got that?"

He grumbles and I feel like I'm dealing with a drunken dog — one that's only partially housebroken. He lurches off to bed and leaves me with the booze and my dirty secret.

At each next destination, each next signing, I've been adrenalized to the hilt, ready for my next big career boost. Now that I think of it, though, yeah, if she's gonna do it, she's gonna do it in LA or New York.

My money's on New York.

MOON KISS

Anne Sipos

Her rainy yell lowered, divulging galaxies.
She electrified doubts, searing gravity,
yielding golden nectar rain.
Night timidly yielded dewy youth,
then, *knowing gentle love.*

THE LAST ACCUSER
Darryl Willis

I feel impact of stone upon
the soles of feet as the ground
reverberates with their fall.
They fall. (I fell so long ago).
I don't recall a day I felt
clean. Used — abused by men
so often all the leering faces
fade to one demonic sneer:
a violent visage holding self
above, judging and condemning.

I do not know what happened to
the one who promised love for me.
His face mutates, transforms into
this mass of hideous, hateful eyes
surrounding me, accusing me,
calling for the penalty.

Now, before *this* man I'm thrown:
a ragged rabbi so unlike
the men whom I have seen before.
I feel their countless eyes that burn
through and past my broken soul.
I know their hate is more for him
than for me — this one who stoops
and with his finger writes in sand.
Their question is impossible:
Ignore or to obey the law?

My eyes look down, I wait for death.
I cringe; I hear my ragged breath.
Then I feel impact of stone
fall to the ground. I am alone.
One by one accusers leave,
when I look up there's only me
and him, the one who writes in sand.

Another word — this one for me,
the last accuser to set free.
Something falls to the ground
as I get up and turn around.
I see my feet and in the sand
the bloody rock that was in my hand.

TOMORROW
Michelle Monet

Tomorrow
I want to go
sit
on the edge of the Universe

I want to dangle

my feet
in a stream of gold

I want to marvel

at the
mauve and taupe earth colors

Tomorrow
I want to sunbathe
on the furthest mountain top

stare into the water
watch it laugh

flowing like

rainbow rapids
I want to smile at trees

and allow them to heal me

Tomorrow
I want to

listen to river rocks

breathing
and feel the sand caress

my toes

Tomorrow
I want to marvel
at the moon
and

get lost in the
cozy clouds

Tomorrow
I will

lose myself —

in the earth

originally published in *Word Explosion © 2017*

THE BRIDGE THAT HOLDS OUR MARGINS
Nuno Ricardo

The bridge that holds our margins remains undone
unfinished pillars hold our ego fed by wounds
amulets of love are being shattered one by one
while hell exposes underrated living rooms.

Drowned in tides that rise too high
for hope new ports can bring some comfort
where rides which burn the boat at every crossing
are lessons mastered with the smallest effort.

Posterity finds many spaces for hesitations
in shadows of our unforsaken history
we were two maps with different scales,
our compasses fine-tuned at faulty symmetry.

This ship has sailed, it belongs now to the sea,
left behind you'll find the unforgetful shore,

all I can do is stand wandering at the pier
waving goodbye like there was a bridge before.

ÁINE

Heath Houston

Wild languages, spake you and I
in meadows where the fairfolk hide
and wilder beasts who calmly bide
for you, their queen, with lowered eyes

"With me, beloved," you pulled me nigh,
"I promise you the bluest sky
that you've to see, and then we'll lie,
our kisses laced with lanquid sighs."

We danced for what seemed long as days
in verdant grass our bodies lay,
skin warmed by sunlight's summer blaze
we wove ourselves like braided snakes

"Please stay with me," my voice was dire,
said breathlessly, my skin afire
as late sun's cinnabar retires,
a reverence to the moon inspired

"We have today," you said to me,
so gentle, so insistently,
your pale skin gold as honeyed wheat
by setting sun's own alchemy

We lay like tigers in the grass,
love spent, aroused, and spent at last,
by midnight's spectral lūmen cast
each moment savored 'fore it passed

In rhythmic breathing, there we lay,
my fingers memorized your face,
soon drowsing in our doomed embrace
our smiles on intimate display

I woke to morning's light at last
no sign of my fair summer lass,
left mourning, our brief moment past,
my goddess in the summer grass.

FRIDAYS

Pedro Jacob

Friday evening he drove to the old printworks. It was a quiet area where abandoned warehouses were a haven to all those too ashamed to expose their demons in the light.

Away from the neon signs and sequined dresses in the fancier parts of the town, he picked up the weekend's entertainment. His usual contact was out of the game, and the new dealer was shady but unthreateningly so.

The week had been long, and he needed a hit before the stressful drive back. After deciding to hide the goods under the spare tire in the trunk of his departed father's El Dorado, he took a hit with the car keys.

Just like that, the burden of his existence lightened up. The canals unveiled a tranquillity hitherto hidden. The persistent fog which had plagued his rut covered the deserted buildings. The sadness of their walls was now unknown. The souls who dwelled inside were lost, fortified from public view.

This feeling came and went in the time it took him to smoke a cigarette. He was soon on the road, driving below the limit to keep the law's wandering eyes at bay.

Most of the drive was uneventful, as he expected it to be. However, the bar district elicited his usual panic routine. His rationalisation compelled him to meet his dealer at a busy hour when the authorities would have their hands full with other public vices.

He saw a police car parked at the end of the promenade which he had to drive past. The sweat overflowed from his brow onto the steering wheel. He wiped it away with his right arm, noticing the mark it left on his jacket sleeve. Salt, water and leather don't go well together.

Without seeing whether or not the officers were in the car, the vehicle plagued his thoughts in the 45-minute drive home. When the panic had subsided, and he could now make out clear images of streets he drove on, a siren sent his heart to his throat.

The blues and reds clouded his environment with the blasted noise marking the beat at which his blood was pumped to his head. In an act of meek surrender, he swerved onto the pavement and halted the car.

This is it, he thought.

With his eyes closed and hands on the wheel, he began to concoct an elaborate excuse for the 5 grams under the spare tire. The sirens changed, and he opened his eyes.

This hadn't been it. An ambulance whizzed past him on more pressing matters. He sighed and chuckled and praised the Lord, not knowing which had happened of his own volition.

The excitement left him as he locked the front door behind him. The flat was messy because it had always been so. After he warmed up a small plate in the oven, he poured himself four fingers of the cheapest whisky he found at the convenience store a few hours earlier. He emptied what his eye-o-meter decided was a gram onto the plate. His paranoia took care of turning the oven off and reminded him to check after he'd sat down.

With an expired gym card, he racked up two generous lines that disappeared into his nose without a trace. He took a generous sip from his drink and leapt onto the balcony to chain-smoke in the company of the nihilists and the third-rate philosophers trapped in his mind.

In the flat below, his neighbour alternated folk with bluegrass. He got used to the fiddler's various styles. His flatmate was out.

The apartment was his kingdom, the weekend his subject. A few lines in, the euphoria abated, and the police car came back to his thoughts.

Unable to resist the realisation, he analysed why it was there, right in the mid-point between his house and his designated meeting spot.

He was towards the end of a very long list of characters who should be forced to reckon with the law on drug-related matters.

And yet, what if the system was genuinely hellbent on destroying the little guy? That's what he heard in some commentary news programme, and surely those people know what they're talking about.

What had happened to his regular dealer? He tried to remember but he couldn't.

What if the new guy had been planted there. He'd only been back for a couple of hours. Maybe there was still time to surrender before the police came.

What if they were already marching up his apartment block, ready to nail him on possession charges?

What if there was a big bald old-timer in prison waiting to possess and nail him at will?

There was no time to waste. He racked up four lines which could have delineated the borders of an old empire. They soon disappeared.

The rest, he flushed. The fiddling of his downstairs neighbour set the pace for his paranoia.

The weekend still awaited him, but he was no longer its king.

SKIN AND SPIRIT

for Heath

Hannah Smit

Careful —
you're becoming
one of my favourite things.

In all your many mysteries
lyrical elegies
serendipities
coy cosmic coffee beans,
I can't think of another thing
that opens so easily
these shuttered parts of me.

You make me smile,
sometimes daydreaming
about a Saturday sleep-in
where I've all but burrowed into you
smelling the unique mix
of your skin and *Spirit,*
breathing it in
and trying to hold it.

How do you make me feel
so girlishly innocent
and wildly inappropriate
at the same time?

I crave your kisses, now,
more than chocolate
and you should know —
I really love chocolate,

but chocolate never made me go warm
from my nose to my toes
like those kisses of yours,
no sir.

I prefer *you.*
(*though I plan on having both*)

RED SKY MORNING
Molly Vaclav

Highs and lows are the way it goes;
the tide of life ebbs and flows.

I was standing knee deep,
stationary to each wave's sweep.
From sky to land and land to sea,
there was no place I'd rather be.

And I stood,
when the salt stung
and the storms raged
and the fish bit at my skin,

And I stood
through every tidal wave,
I never would have given in.

My heart is made of leather,
it can take a little weather.
If you think that's the reason I left,
then you should know me better.

Yes,
passion
has an ugly side.

It's a bulldozer voice
that plows through you, mid-sentence.
It's a seething rage
for the slow, minimum-wage cashier.
It's a hurricane of hurt
that turns, never-ending,
torn up by all the worst things, without wisps of mending.

But passion
also
looks like
your hands holding mine during a cold night.

It smells like
the coffee you brought me at each morning light.
It tastes like
snowflakes at the top of tall mountain Blue.
And it feels like
your hugs after
too
many
days without you.

You're a cold drink
in the dusty summer sun,
refreshingly thoughtful,
and ready for a run.

And you're a subtle wink,
a playful dance in the kitchen,
funny kisses on the cheek,
and being sneakily smitten.

And I would take
the good and bad
without question of a doubt,
because the good was wonderful,
I never wanted to live without.

And then
deep
in my heart
a seed of anger
began to start.

My fuse of patience had been whittled short;
a semblance of attitude began to form.
I learned how to talk over people too,
and negative fixations would soak and brew.

That
was enough.

As much as I could love you,
(and it's from sea to shining sea),
I couldn't let that darkness
become a part of me.

I am not blind.
The storms
have
lessened over time.
You have made

strong strides
to better your design.

And you are smart
And you are kind
And there's no doubt in my mind
that you will find
yourself
exactly where you want to be,
if you decide it's what you need.

But I can't be here right now.
I need to get back to me.
I need to salvage what I've got before I lose a piece.

Please recognize that through my eyes
you're everything you could be.
To say I thought you weren't enough,
you do misrepresent me.

DRIFTWOOD HEART
a poem in eleven haiku
Michelle Muses

Moonlight breaks from clouds.
I stand barefoot in the waves,
watching the ocean,

letting the sea breeze
take me back to carefree days
when I was a child:

sizzling summers spent
on swings draped with wisteria,
gliding through crisp air,

breathing in scents of
lilacs gone wild after rains,
unfurling in wind,

falling asleep to
sand glittering in my hair,
on pillows, in dreams.

The yearning in me
fans open and then ripples
into the vast sea,

embraced by currents
splashing forth, wave after wave,

sparkling in moonlight.

Let driftwood hearts be.
Nostalgia will come to it's
own nameless ocean,

calling, calling out,
and hear it's echoes in the
roar of throbbing seas.

Ever the wistful
sojourner, my heart will ride
the waves with courage,

find a home not in
just one place but everywhere
it dares to wander.

PAINTING THE MUSE

Jeffrey Valencia

I am tired of trying to look inward
only to find nothing in the interior.

The blemishes and scars printed on my neurons
Have escaped me, I spend so
much time trying to be in touch,
I lose touch
At the slightest moment, I'm gone.

High from earlier, painting on my canvas
Until something appears in front of me
I pour my letters on to a sheet.

I wake up and carry myself through the door
To come back and work;
that fulfills an empty jar with cracks
on the circumference.

COLOGNE
Aaska Ejaz

A cool breeze spread your fragrance
my heart caught and I breathed deeply
my senses awoke~my nostrils, in familiarity,
a longing sweat beads my forehead.

The tremble of my hands, nerves stimulated,
Tick~tocks of your shoes, quickening my pulse,
plucked my heartstrings and provoked a rhyme,
The sound of your laugh whispered in my ears,
Sparked the heat of my imagination.

Suddenly, my steps, falling faster toward,
My eyes veiled now in colors of the heavens,
Lie a magnificent rainbow of love shone
creating your image before me.

I opened the door, finally,
you came back to me.

THE MIRACULOUS BIRTH
A Religious Satire
C. E. Hammock

When the Messiah was being born at a second rate community hospital outside of Buffalo New York, the evangelicals erected flashing signs with arrows pointing the way, while angels sang overhead in the beams of spinning spotlights borrowed from a used car lot.

Maria had found herself unexpectedly pregnant one day, soon after her engagement to her future husband Joe. It was quite a surprise considering that she was still a virgin. Joe accused her of having an affair with Larry, who had been chasing after her for several years, but Maria considered him crude and embarrassing, and rejected all of his advances. She finally convinced Joe of her faithfulness but was at a loss to explain the pregnancy. She did remember this weird dream she had one night about a dove wrapping its wings around her and talking naughty into her ear. That was back around Easter. She didn't remember what the dove said, but she was shocked and embarrassed when she awoke.

During the birth sweet fragrances of roses and lilacs, and honeysuckle and jasmine pervaded the room. From the divinely chosen vagina proceeded beams of heavenly light through which the child emerged. An attending angel called out: "Bring forth the platter," and an entourage of seraphim descended from the sky bringing a golden platter and pure white linen upon which the child was delivered. The baby emerged, its hands folded in prayer; his eyes cast down in contemplation of his perfect deity.

The birth was attended by a poet, a priest and a politician. The politician took the opportunity to be photographed with the divine mother. The next day the photograph was emblazoned across every major paper, with headlines like: "Politician Brings New Word into the World," "God's Country Graced with New Messiah," and "Newest Divine Baby Born."

The poet commemorated the event with such lines as: "Here comes forth / on this day / a new wonder / without parallel / the joy of all mankind / and a wonder to behold," and other such doggerel. The priest simply fainted from joy.

Adoption offers rolled in from all around the world, offering to raise the child in comfortable homes that Maria and Joe couldn't afford, being poor. Pious families that would give the child a proper religious training and distract from the fact that the child was technically "illegitimate," since Maria and Joe were in fact not yet married. Even mega-churches, Jehovah's Witnesses', and the Mormons in Salt Lake City, all competed for Maria and Joe's attention to take on the burden of the child and raise him to fulfill the apocalyptic expectations of their respective faiths.

With all the fanfare and excitement outside the little community hospital, the board of directors used this miraculous birth as an opportunity for fund-raising, allowing the new family to stay in the hospital with free accommodations until the board could arrange an international press conference and hit up some big donors.

Following the birth, the new mother was allowed to rest and bond with her new baby. Inside the hospital, water turned into wine and flowed out of faucets and shower heads, at first frightening the nurses who thought it might be blood, until one tasted it and realized it was a really nice Bordeaux. The hospital had to bring in outside drinking water so patients wouldn't get drunk.

One morning, the halls were overrun with bleating lambs and bunny rabbits with fluffy tails rushing into the nursery to kiss and lick the new baby. The baby giggled and cooed under the warm lips of the lambs and the soft bunny tongues and blessed the animals before the security guards could shoo them away.

Other miracles happened: cancer patients went into remission, crippled children began to walk on their own, and ghostly spirits of the dead that hung around the place, sought release from their wonderings, and disappeared through light radiating apertures in the walls into their afterlife.

The nurses became fixated on the baby's poop schedule. They soon realized how considerate the new baby was for his mother, only pooping moments before she changed the diaper. If mom slept too long between diaper changes, the baby would discreetly hold his poop until she was ready. The nurses were diligent in disposing of the soiled diapers and divided the poop up in back rooms for their own personal use. By the end of the first week, there was already over 200 lbs of magic baby poop sold on eBay with many customers complaining that it smelled bad and was making people who ate it sick.

When the day of the press conference arrived, the little auditorium was crammed full of cameras and reporters. The divine family sat at the front of the room, like a tableau or an image from an icon. The baby lay in his mother's arms glowing with light while subtle beams radiated from his eyes, casting circles of white light on the ceiling, which appeared and disappeared as the baby opened and closed his eyes. Tiny angels flew in circles over the baby's head forming a golden halo; another angel held a golden platter behind the mother's head.

When the questions began, the first thing the reporters wanted to know was: what is the new baby's name? Maria proudly announced that they decided to name him Josh. A murmuring stirred through the crowd, with lots of head-nodding and general agreement that Josh was a good name.

Some of the female reporters were curious about how the delivery went: was it painful? Maria answered shyly, while blushing: it was pretty easy, actually rather "pleasurable" she said, putting her hand over her mouth in embarrassment. "I think I might have had a few orgasms."

How did you know you were pregnant? Since you never had sex before? "Well I had this strange dream about a giant dove coming and talking dirty to me, while we floated on a white cloud surrounded by olive trees," Maria told them. "And after my periods stopped, I went and peed on a pregnancy stick and it turned blue."

One of the male reporters, trying to bolster his masculinity in the manly presence of Joe, asked: how will he protect the child from those who might want to do the baby harm. "You know, those atheist and crazy cult people?" Joe said his brothers and cousins will help him with their shotguns and rifles. Simon, Andy, and James were already waiting outside in case there was any trouble. John, Phil and Matt were getting their home ready. His brother Thomas, who complained a lot, was, unfortunately, unreliable.

A reporter from the National Inquirer, who was investigating the baby poop scandal, wanted to know if the eBay poop was real. Maria said the nurses take care of that, but she didn't really think it was her baby's poop, after all, 200 lbs of poop is a lot for one little baby to make in just a week, and besides her baby's poop doesn't stink: "It actually smells like roses and lilacs."

THE BRIDGE
Gosia Rokicka

she's there, on the other end —
tip-toeing nervously
throwing sparkling glances
and leftover smiles /
scratching the surface
of the ancient stone that reads
"Come in. Forever"

the sun, a ripe orange
the river, a red wine
the air, an aloe vera scent

I can't go with you, I say,
not this time, not any more —
you need to be brave
confident
calm
capable of making the right choices

that never happened before, she says

her eyes, wet stones
my hand, a willow in the wind
the bridge, a shadow in the rain

I'm still standing there,
waiting for the rainbow to appear.

FOUR SEASONS
Shaleen Rakesh

There are two things
I forgot to tell you

the first had to do
with the biting chill of winter
and the second with the way
the colours run in spring

I forgot to tell you
because I only knew you
in the summer and the fall
the time of long days and pretty sunsets.

CUTTING DIAMONDS WITH AN EXHALE
DH Bogucki

facets framing beams
into a cathedral of awareness
sheltering hearts in a nave
light an idol
worshiped by the breath

JUST FOR ONE DAY
James Hanna-Magill

If I could, my words would

F
A
L
L on the page and

R U N. But they

Mask,
Deny ME and
Dissemble.

They

E off the page and
S
I
R

T U R N. In layers

Immobile,
Let ME be
Lucid.

Just for one day.

All was potential
Before I fell
HARD,
Led blindly in
Etched out ways.

N O L O N G E R. But

When I rise, not if,
In MY new world
gentler,
Lucent, edgeless, I'
Ll see why I erred and try

A G A I N.

One day.

MEMOIR
Lyndsay Knowles

I step back
and try to find it.

The truth of this story.

To see each angle,
embellishment,
edit and cut.

Lost in the pages,
unable to find my way out.

I look for the cracks,
the omissions
in the words of each line.

And I wonder —

Who owns the stories
we tell of our lives?

Whose truth
does this story reveal?

THE ANDROID OPTION

Ash Gray

Our daughter is dead," sneered Qwellvin EyNdo, "and you sing and hum on the night of her funeral?"

Morvellik EyNdo ignored her wife, pursing her dark blue lips into a kiss as she slowly reapplied black lipstick. In the white overhead light of the restroom, her blue skin was practically glowing, swathed as it was in a long black gown, sleeveless, with a black fur wrapped around her naked shoulders. Her eye was large and violet and was glittering with mirth in the center of her forehead, just above the bridge of the sloping, almost non-existent nose that melted into her face. She hummed an upbeat tune as she dropped the lipstick in her triangular purse and adjusted the mass of squirming tentacles that sat piled atop her head like drowsy worms.

The two women were alone in the public restroom, its black floors and walls gleaming like polished mirrors to reflect them tenfold. Because the enziri were a mono-gendered race, the sign on the other side of the door was not symbolic of sex but of age. Those enziri one thousand years and older were allowed to enter the restroom in which the bickering married couple currently stood.

A very elderly enziri, drooping with wrinkles like crepe, had just left the room after asking Qwellvin to sign a digital copy of Fallen Stars. Unable to help herself, Qwellvin took a stylus from behind her pointed ear and signed the digital book, smiling and joking all the while, blithely basking in the glow of literary success. She couldn't help feeling dirty when the elderly woman had gleefully gone.

"You sicken me," muttered Qwellvin, though she

wondered if she was really speaking to herself.

"Why should I mourn? You aren't," accused Morvellik, eye glaring sharply at Qwellvin through the mirror. Her bandaged hand — broken from an innocent hand game with Xenu — shook as she reapplied mascara to eyelashes that reached incredibly long from her large eye. "Little Qwell was your daughter, not mine," she said bitterly, "and Xenu isn't even alive."

Qwellvin swallowed and stared at the floor, across which her blue tail-tentacles were sadly squirming from the back of her suit.

Morvellik was infertile and was thus incapable of continuing the endless replication of the Ndo line. Within enziri society, it was a matter of great shame, and within the EyNdo marriage, it was an unfortunate reality that had shaken the two women almost to the brink of divorce.

Enziri could only birth one daughter in their lifetime and every enziri gave birth to a daughter that was identical to her in every way. Incarnationism, their planet's most widely accepted religion, believed the involuntary birth process to be an endless replication of the self, a preservation of the original inhabitants of Planet Indira. Thus, the only real death happened to those who could not produce offspring.

The daughters of a married couple were always fated to wed, as the Originals had been married in the days of Ancient Indira. Little Qwell would have been expected to marry Xenu one day, the prospect of which was another scandal all its own. Qwellvin felt a fool for thinking she could buy an android child which would solve all their problems.

No matter what they did, Qwellvin and Morvellik were at fault and they were bad parents and the public hated them. They were expected to lie down and allow the android child to innocently trample them as it fumbled its way through their lives, until their bones were broken and their walls stained with blood, and if they uttered a word of discontent, they were lambasted yet again in every publication on the planet. They were widely viewed as having brought their own misery upon themselves, and "Serves them right for adopting a mechanical abomination!" was the prevalent attitude. Eventually, they became the go-to example of what happens to those who scorn ancient tradition for new-age gobbledygook.

Those who didn't sneer and turn their noses up at what had been deemed "the EyNdo scandal" were sociologists, psychologists, and behaviorists, who were keenly interested in the social development of an android child, especially one that was being raised by two celebrities in the public eye. The EyNdo family was constantly extended invitations to appear on talk shows, podcasts, reality shows, and to participate in experiments for obscene amounts of quillicks. It did a great deal to skyrocket their careers at the expense of and to the detriment of their very souls.

Because of Xenu and the entire tragedy surrounding her, Morvellik was being offered great roles for the first time in centuries, while Qwellvin had never sold as many copies of Fallen Stars in all one hundred and seventy-five years it had been published. Now suddenly, the book was flying off the physical and digital shelves. She felt dirty every time she received another notification, announcing that thousands more quillicks had been dumped in her account. It was blood money. From her own child's death had blossomed her lifelong dream. It was at once her worst nightmare and her greatest desire, manifested into the most bittersweet reality. She loathed being in her skin every second of every day and yet could not ignore the happy fans who had discovered her work as a result of the tragedy of her child's violent murder.

After all that had happened, Qwellvin now fully understood that taking the android option had been a tragic, inescapably stupid mistake.

Qwellvin sadly checked her wristwatch, knowing they would have to attend family counseling as soon as the funeral rites for Little Qwell had concluded. Outside, the traditional chorus dressed in solemn blue robes was still singing, all crowded on a hovering platform, their magnetic boots holding them to it against the lack of gravity on Damara, Indira's second moon. Little Qwell's body rested in an upright star cube, her frozen face calm and emotionless in the small window of the lid. When the singing had completed, the cube would launch into the stars.

Qwellvin knew people were probably whispering and muttering in disapproval that she and Morvellik were not outside, prostrate across the barren, rocky ground with grief. Hands in the pockets of her blazer, she sagged where she stood.

Morvellik yawned, "Maybe I won't go back, just head over to my masseur. She has a practice on Damara now."

"You helped raise Little Qwell, your heartless crizpaw," Qwellvin hissed, "The least you can do is attend her damned funeral."

Morvellik laughed her tinkling laugh, though there was a trill of sadness to it, "And yet you stand here with me, avoiding the same wretched fate of phony mourning, of forced tears. Don't delude yourself, my darling Qwellvin. Don't pretend. I think we are both immeasurably relieved to have the matter over," She blinked sadly and whispered, "Little Qwell is dead. She no longer has to endure our clumsy parenting. It's a mercy, really. I think she would thank Xenu if she could, and perhaps we should as well."

"Don't be dramatic," said Qwellvin at once and rolled her eye, "We weren't perfect parents, but we weren't that bad either."

Morvellik cocked a brow, "Is that what you tell yourself so you can sleep every night, dear? I spent all day, every day drunk beside the pool, while you were constantly hunched at a computer screen, typing away stories that were more important to you than Little Qwell, admit it. You never wanted to be a mother, while I always wanted nothing more," Her lip trembled as she whispered, "Funny how life works out, isn't it?"

"Hysterical," muttered Qwellvin tonelessly.

"Stop pretending to care. The media storm surrounding this has done nothing but launch your ridiculous little novel into the stratosphere," went on Morvellik with sneering disdain, "Everyone wants to read the book written by the woman whose ancient and powerful bloodline was ended by the evil of an unfeeling machine. The Ey line ends with you because of what Xenu did. You are now a prime example of what horrors technology can bring to the modern enziri's life. How was your interview on Indira Today, by the way?"

Qwellvin seethed. "I only agreed to the interview because it was an opportunity to protest the further distribution of those — things!" she erupted furiously.

"Right," sighed Morvellik, unconvinced, "because it wasn't enough that you sued the kid factory for every last quillick they were worth — "

Qwellvin's eye popped, and she took a halting step into the room. "You think this is about money?" she sneered, "Well, you're wrong. This was never about money! Our daughter was murdered by one of those talking toasters, and it's our moral obligation to let other parents know what exactly it is they're bringing into their home! Mor . . . the damn thing crushed her. Like stepping on a bug."

Morvellik's lip trembled but she said nothing as she adjusted her earring in the mirror.

"Could you live with yourself if we never spoke up and another fake kid killed a real one?" Qwellvin went on, eye on the floor.

"Yes, I could," said Morvellik at once, and Qwellvin glared at her through the mirror. Morvellik sniffed imperiously, "Especially since you spent half our fortune to have this dismal funeral on the moon. Little Qwell always wanted to visit Damara, didn't she? Now . . . she'll have her wish." The last words were low and bitter. Primping completed, Morvellik gathered her skirts in one hand and clicked on lethal high heels out the bathroom door, chin lifted, hips sashaying until the large bow riding her backside drifted on the air behind her.

Qwellvin was following, when she heard one of the stall doors slowly open and she froze where she stood. A pair of purple high heels stepped down from the toilet on which their owner had been squatting and an enziri appeared around the stall door, stepping with a smirk into the white glow of the overhead lights. Qwellvin instantly recognized her as the same journalist who had been hounding her for weeks since the murder. She was very short and slender, and was always rumpled from sleepless haste. Her necktie was loose, her shirt half untucked, her head-tentacles coming free of their wormy bun. She had lines under her eye and dark circles framing her eyelids, and Qwellvin knew immediately she had ridden all night on a moon shuttle just to make it to Damara and the funeral, just so she could position herself in the restroom, in the precise spot she needed to be in order to eavesdrop on the mourning parents. Her name was Llori Vorz, and Qwellvin had to admire her resolve, even if it was damned annoying.

Llori Vorz adjusted her tight skirt and blazer and clicked on shapely legs toward Qwellvin, who stood frozen with rage near the row of sinks. To Qwellvin's horror, the journalist quietly pulled a small, cylindrical device from her oval purse and clicked a button on it with a long purple nail. Qwellvin's voice buzzed from the recorder, "Our daughter is dead, and you sing and hum on the night of her funeral? You sicken me."

"Why should I mourn? You aren't," answered Morvellik's sneering voice.

Qwellvin tensed furiously, fangs grinding behind her lips when the smug little journalist abruptly clicked off the recording and smiled at her.

"What do you want?" Qwellvin darkly demanded.

"Money, obviously," answered the journalist derisively and turned to the mirror. Qwellvin watched in silent fury as the little woman checked her lipstick.

"My mistake. I should have asked how much you want," sneered Qwellvin.

"Twenty million quillicks," said the journalist, and Qwellvin thought she heard her own appalled brain leave in disgust out the door.

"Ex . . . Excuse me?" managed Qwellvin weakly.

"You heard me," said Llori Vorz, still primping in the mirror, "Twenty million. Or I tell the world just how sorry you aren't that poor Little Qwell was smashed into paste."

Qwellvin glared.

"You will watch helplessly as your career unravels around you," said Llori Vorz casually, "You'll become a pariah again overnight. For what goddess-fearing enziri would ever reject the ecstasy and agony of motherhood, that holiest of holy callings?" She laughed softly.

"I'd have to drop by the bank first," said Qwellvin unhappily, "It's not like I walk around with those kinds of quillicks on me."

"Whatever you have to do," said Llori Vorz darkly, "Get it done. I want my quillicks. I worked hard for them. You don't wanna know what I did to gain access to this side of the moon."

"No, I don't," Qwellvin muttered. She swallowed hard and fumbled out her phone, scrolling with her thumb through the calendar on the oval screen, "Fine. Meet me at . . . at Vana's. It's local."

Llori Vorz snorted, "It's also a strip club. Not a very smart move for someone so conscious about their image."

"Never said we were meeting inside, did I? I'll meet you in the back alley. I give you the quillicks, you give me the recording. And if you make copies — "

"You'll what?" said Llori Vorz at once, lips twisting in amusement, "What could you possibly do?"

"I could kill you," Qwellvin muttered bitterly.

"You realize I'm still recording, right?" said Llori Vorz, unfazed.

Qwellvin clenched her fangs against her own helplessness. She and Morvellik had really dug their own graves this time. How stupid were they to have stood in a public restroom having such a conversation?

Qwellvin continued scrolling through the calendar on her phone, "We can make the drop on . . . Crap. I'm booked for the week. I can't cancel these appointments — "

"Then you can kiss your career goodbye," said Llori and turned for the door.

Qwellvin lunged to block her path. "Wait!" she begged, and Llori halted, impatiently folding her arms.

"I've got to attend . . ." Qwellvin's lip curled, "family counseling tonight. If I leave the funeral early, I can run to the bank before counseling, and if you meet me outside after, we can make the drop."

To Qwellvin's immense relief, Llori's bald brow went up and her bottom lip pushed out in silent agreement. "All right," she said, "You're still seeing Dr. Wr, right? I know where her office is."

"Of course, you do," said Qwellvin darkly.

Llori smirked, hips swaying as she went out the door.

Dr. Wr was a small woman with an annoying way of constantly clearing her throat. She sat in a purple chair shaped like an ice cream scoop, one leg crossed over the other as she peered over her spectacles, reading a glowing datapad. Qwellvin, Morvellik, and Xenu sat in similar half-egg chairs, silently waiting for the session to begin.

Qwellvin kept checking her watch. They had been sitting there for ten minutes in silence, and she thought she would combust. She was terrified she would be late leaving the session, and then Llori Vorz would splash that damned recording all over the interweb. Thanks to the gaggle of eager fans who had the audacity to bombard her after the funeral, she hadn't been able to make it to the bank. The digi-check was inside her blazer, made out to the despicable little woman and ready to be cashed. Her hands shook every time she thought of having to hand over so many quillicks. And all to keep her career alive, to firmly keep intact the feeling that she was a brilliant and successful writer.

"Stop checking your watch, Qwell, for the sake of the goddess," muttered Morvellik, whose hand was tossed back on her wrist to hold an e-cig, "It's just one hour. You can't talk about your feelings for one hour?"

Qwellvin stopped checking her watch and fidgeted with her long fingers instead, locked in a private hell of anxiety. She hadn't told Morvellik about the journalist on the shuttle over. She was still wondering if she shouldn't just hire a hit on the woman. Would be less expensive anyway.

Xenu sat in a chair between Qwellvin and Morvellik, straight and still, hands calmly folded in her lap, as if they were yet more objects she must keep in precise order. She was wearing a long, straight dress with geometric weaving on the front, the sleeves of which each hooked on her middle fingers. In the wake of Little Qwell's death, the dress was unashamedly yellow, and Xenu was even wearing a rainbow of color around her throat in the form of a glowing digi-necklace.

"Xenu and I had a little chat before the two of you arrived," said Dr. Wr, not looking up from her datapad. Her lips quivered somberly as she said, "Xenu, I want you to tell your parents what you told me."

Qwellvin and Morvellik both looked at Xenu. Morvellik's large eye was hooded and weary, while Qwellvin's mind was still with Llori Vorz.

Xenu hesitated bitterly, then without looking at either parent, she announced, "I destroyed Little Qwell so you would love me!"

There was silence in the room. Morvellik's tired expression barely changed except that she sniffed, then took a long pull on her e-cig. Qwellvin was anxiously staring off and didn't appear to hear what was said.

"Did you hear what I said?!" Xenu demanded.

Neither parent answered.

"See!" shouted the android, lunging out of her chair, "This is what I'm talking about! It's like I'm not even alive!"

"You aren't, honey," said Morvellik tiredly. She ignored it when the child gave her a menacing look and instead kissed out smoke. "Sit back down," she said, eye lazily drifting away.

Xenu swallowed angrily and sat back down.

It took Qwellvin a minute to realize there had been an outburst and another minute to realize Dr. Wr was looking at her. Qwellvin cleared her throat in shame.

"Did you hear what your daughter said, Mrs. EyNdo?" asked Dr. Wr calmly. She set the datapad on her lap and pressed each three-fingered hand together in a steeple.

"I . . . no," Qwellvin admitted, scratching her nose.

Dr. Wr sighed, "Your child clearly murdered the other as a plea for attention, for your love."

"It's not healthy to bend to tantrums, doc," said Morvellik, lazy-eyed and uncaring.

"And that mode of thinking is why Xenu's tantrums have

escalated to murder," answered Dr. Wr.

Morvellik sneered, and Qwellvin went still in her chair.

"Excuse me, what?" Qwellvin demanded, blinking angrily.

"Oh, heard that, did you?" mocked Dr. Wr in disgust.

"What the hell do you know about parenting?" Qwellvin demanded.

"Not a damned thing," added Morvellik, kissing out smoke.

"Do you even have kids?" Qwellvin demanded.

"They never have kids," added Morvellik, kissing out more smoke.

Dr. Wr sighed tiredly, "The two of you can tag team me, but the fact remains that your child felt unloved in the household. Talk to her."

Qwellvin regained her composure and adjusted her tie, glancing sideways at Xenu. The child was glaring at the wall and wouldn't look at her. Qwellvin cleared her throat. "Xenu . . . honey," she said softly. She reached over, and after hesitating, took the little android's cold, hard hand in her own.

Xenu refused to look at Qwellvin for another beat, but realizing the woman had no intention of letting her go, her head grudgingly rotated on her neck, the mechanical pigtails flowing up and then down.

"We didn't love Little Qwell more than you," said Qwellvin gently.

Xenu's lip trembled, "R-Really?"

"Really," said Morvellik just as gently, and leaning over, she smiled and rubbed Xenu's shoulder.

"We neglected you both about the same," said Qwellvin warmly.

Morvellik smiled and nodded, rubbing the little girl's back.

"I . . . I think I feel better," Xenu realized.

As Dr. Wr looked on in shock, Qwellvin and Morvellik hugged the little android child, who sobbed in the midst of their warm affection and hugged them back with arms that trembled.

"I'm so sorry I destroyed her!" Xenu sobbed, "I just wanted you to love me!"

"It's all right, sweetheart, it's all right," whispered Morvellik, who was crying freely as she kissed the child's head.

"We'll take you to the fair after this," said Qwellvin, crying hard, "You can ride on the moon cars all you want. How's that sound?"

"Yay!" squealed Xenu.

"No! This is wrong, dammit!" shouted Dr. Wr, who'd had enough. She leapt out of her chair and came out of her high heel, dropping the datapad in the process. It clattered to the floor and its light snapped out.

The three EyNdos broke apart, blinking at the woman in surprise.

"What is it? I thought we were making good progress," said a baffled Morvellik. She looked at her wife, "Didn't you?"

"Yeah," agreed Qwellvin with a shrug, "No one threw chairs this time."

"What the hell kind of parenting is this?" Dr. Wr demanded, offering her pale blue palms, "You admit to being crap parents and then reinforce disturbing behavior? I should call social services and have this child taken away — !"

"Just try it!" shouted Morvellik, springing from her chair.

Qwellvin rose to her feet, glaring at Dr. Wr. "Come on, sweetheart. We don't have to take this," she said and offered her hand to Xenu, who took it with a dreamy smile.

Outside, journalists were loitering with hover cams, waiting for the famous family to emerge. Spotting the EyNdos, they swept forward at once in a cloud. The family ran and had almost made it to their hover car when Llori Vorz rounded the corner and grabbed Qwellvin's arm. The journalist had a greedy glint in her eye when she offered her hand and hissed in Qwellvin's ear, "Well?"

Qwellvin miserably reached inside her blazer.

"What's this about?" Morvellik demanded in disgust.

Qwellvin didn't answer. She sneered as she pulled out the digi-check, and with a trembling hand, she offered it to Llori Vorz. The journalist triumphantly snatched the digi-check and tucked it in her purse, turning away, "Glad doing business with you!"

Qwellvin scowled. "Wait a damn minute!" she shouted. "Give me the recording!"

"Recording?" repeated Morvellik sharply. "Qwell, what the hell is going on?"

Qwellvin didn't have a chance to answer. Xenu stepped forward and called, "You dropped this, lady!"

Llori Vorz turned to face them with an uncertain frown. Xenu was offering her closed hand. Patting herself and wondering what she could have dropped, the journalist drew closer and reached out — and screamed in shrill pain when Xenu grabbed her hand, crushing every bone in it. She watched in wide-eyed horror as white bones split from her blue flesh, spattering her face in a sudden sprinkle of blood.

As the crowd of journalists swept over, Xenu quickly let go. "Oh, no!" she wailed with award winning sorrow, "I'm so sorry!"

Llori Vorz shrieked and sobbed, stepping out of her shoe and dropping her purse as she fled.

The journalists pressed in, hover cams clicking away as they shouted questions. The happy family drew close together, faces spread with phony smiles, and Qwellvin discreetly stepped on the fallen purse, crushing the recording device and the digi-check inside.

Basking in the spotlight, Xenu put an innocent finger to her lips and rocked bashfully back and forth.

"Xenu! Xenu! Were you trying to help the woman?" a journalist called.

"Do you feel guilty about hurting her?" called another.

"Was she attacking you?" called yet another, "And would you be willing to star in a film about the incident?"

"Would your mother be willing to star in it too?" shouted a small journalist in the back.

"Morvellik! Morvellik, over here! Smile for the camera, beautiful!"

"Qwellvin! Qwellvin! Are you going to write a book about what happened here? Qwellvin!"

Qwellvin and Morvellik stood either side of Xenu, the

proud parents each clasping her shoulders.

"This is going to be great for our careers," muttered Morvellik through her fixed smile.

"I know," muttered Qwellvin through her own.

OF FIRE AND WORDS

DiAmaya Dawn

Of fire
And lust you're made,
For you breathe enigmas
Of new beginnings but covert
Your thoughts
Sly words
You blow to me — they burn my skin
Boil my blood, and you watch
Still, for you're made
Of fire

THE WORN PAGES
of words and lives
Allan 'Alto' Rae

Dusty bookstores holding shelves
leading to corridors winding into
infinite bindings hard and soft where
each edition holds a life, a story, some
familiar, most not.

Chronicles of sacred text on worn pages
paying homage to lives past and present.
It is the inextricable sound of snow falling
on a frozen pond, so faint, almost lost.

Almost.

In each of these, a dream, a hope, a want
a need, a fear; glances at our seminal being
raw and wide for the taking by thirsty eyes
yearning quench.

Here they stand side by side, searing glances
into the universal truth of where we live.
Let me fill my pages with words from yours
and yours with words from mine.

HOPE
Furaha 'Orisirisi' Asani

Hope died
and she took with her all of your pride

so that you were forced down to your knees
and fear became your crippling disease

and it plunged its talons deep within
and made cynicism your darkest sin

but the only faith you'd need
didn't have to be bigger than a mustard seed

and because you held onto the last drop of love within you
it watered the seed and a new sprig of hope grew.

BLUEBERRY HILL

Efe Nakpodia

Through the formless gates
of the city with no walls,
she finally appeared.

In this dream, I was the king,
and she was my blueberry queen.
At dawn, she smiled at me, then
gave me the sun. Suddenly,
the city started to shake
and I started to burn.

Awoken by the rose pink light
of day, it dawned on me that
the lady of my sweet dreams
was a princess from a place
called Faraway.

Nevertheless, I shall see her
flawless face again. Tonight,
I will lay down on Blueberry Hill,
blink twice, and fall asleep.

Again.

MOON-KISSED

Tasneem Kagalwalla

Soft wafts of brilliant white caress her breath
ashore I, salvaged, lie as time stands still
translucent ebbs and flows, as she fulfills
promises that wait her lighted wonder
life poured into dark, cross shimmering waves
to resurrect in calm never ending.

THE ART OF LONELINESS
Joseph Chibike

"Last night, I saw a woman dance to solemn music."
"Solemn music?" I said.
"Like a catholic hymn."
"No way…"
His face shot with excitement.
"I swear, man. She had this old radio set out in the veranda. I think it was *silent night.* Didn't have a care in the world."
"She let herself go," I said.
He nodded. We both smiled.
"Man that's beautiful."
We went silent for a while.
"What about you? Find anything?"
I shrugged.
"Not really."

Loneliness is a form of art. And like all art forms, it has its styles of expression. The catch though, is knowing how the artist has chosen to show craft.

Sometimes, my friend and I would pack our tool kit, and disappear into the night. We'd map our routes extensively, all that planning, so our paths never intercepted.

We'd feature in as many stories as we could find; catch them as they drifted in cold night breeze.

This was serious business. We collected the places we visited, in different colours. Until for us, the city became a rainbow of nocturnal memories.The next morning we'd circle back home, and talk about work.

Loneliness was art; our minds our canvas.

Over time, we had amassed an impressive collection. Little memories of little things.

For me, the best stories were of things even the night didn't offer. Love and romance. Dreams of growing old with a woman with twitchy eyes. Things like that.

There always was the suspicion we kept the best stories from each other.That we hid our masterpieces in private chambers for special memories.

The night before, I met Mr. K.

The old man sat under the broken streetlight, from where he gave music to the night. From his piano leached a thousand memories and dreams; hints of souls trapped in strings and notes.

I walked up to him.

"Don't you feel cold?" I said.

He kept with his music.

I sat down beside him. He smelled of alcohol and harmattan.

"The night. The cold. The loneliness. Why do you play?"

He said nothing.

I stood up to leave.

"I play for the night," he said. " — And the cold…and the loneliness."

"That appears to be something we share," I said.

"What?"

"Loneliness."

I sat down.

We spoke of music and youth. Of dreams and love. Of loneliness.

He told me his story. About a woman in his youth.

She'd fallen in love with his music, and he with her brilliant eyes.

"The way they behaved whenever she spoke of flowers," he said.

"Did they twitch?" I asked.

"Yes!"

His face lit up.

"Would you like to buy flowers?" she said.

Her voice was music.

"I wish I could. I don't think I have enough money," the man said.

She nodded.

"But to be honest, I can't trust myself to take care of them like you do."

She smiled.

"No amount of kind words will get you free flowers," she said.

"Fair enough. I think that'll be good for the flowers. In fact, I think the best way to ensure they survive, is not to sell them. You love them too much."

"And you talk too much," she said.

He shrugged.

"I'll be on my way now."

"Come around again tomorrow," she said.

"So you can defeat me again?"

"Yes."

When he couldn't walk to her place, he wrote. She wrote back.

Then it became a habit. They would write even when they had seen each other the day before.

Short letters — notes, if you will. Footnotes they left each other when time stole pages from the little stories they built together.

One day she even sent flowers with her note.

It said, *"Not for your kind words, but for your kind spirit."*

"She had a beautiful way of fusing memories with gestures," he said.

One day he sent a note.

It said, *"Let's dance, to the rhythm of our heartbeat."*

She wrote back.

It said, *"…but my heart is chaos."*

He wrote a note. She didn't write back.

He never stopped writing her. He never stopped replying the notes he sent her. Not even time could steal this story from him. He was going to tell it, to himself.

The little girl fell on her knees, and mourned.

"Why does nature hate flowers so much?" she said.

"What do you mean?"

"Nature gives quick death to animals. But flowers die slowly, piece by piece. Why do they have to hurt for so long?"

"But are you not missing something?" her mother said.

"What?"

"The love affair between nature and flowers," she said.

"What do you mean?"

"True lovers never let go of each other at once. They do so, slowly, piece by piece, gracefully. Letting go is a rite of passage."

The little girl smiled. Tears descended her cheeks as quickly as her twitching eyes let them.

"They're telling their love story," she said.

"Yes, they are."

The next night, I stayed home. I thought of the people I'd met on other nights. I wondered if they too were artists, showing their craft, and if I had missed their style of expression.

Perhaps I featured in someone's art, too. Perhaps I hang on their wall as a masterpiece — but who am I kidding.

I thought of the solemn dancer, and if she thought herself

a performer. Her veranda her stage, the night breeze her audience.

Mr. K. built parallel universes where his dreams came true. Worlds that lurked between morphemes. Romance trapped in ink.

I thought about the woman I bumped into at the park some nights ago. I wondered if I'd spilled her ink. If I made a mess of her art. I hope she recovers from that.

In a way, we all are artists. Every day, we pack our tool kit, and disappear into a canvas of our loneliness.

KNOWLEDGE

Daphelba DeBeauvoir

I long for ignorance of the divide,
miss the innocence of unity,
for the mind to see through words
out beyond designations
and the titles we burden spirit with
as if an essence so free might be contained,
could be explained in a syllable:

girl! boy! us! them!

objects are given names
to soothe our nature for debate
yet these labels, these definitions
they claim, own, encapsulate
they sort, organize, separate

we come to know too much
while truly knowing nothing at all.

THE BEIRUT BAKER
Parabolical

I don't smell the bread anymore
Nor the furnace it's in
Nor the sea across the road
I don't smell the diesel from the trucks
I don't smell the trash burning
I don't smell the dust in the wind
I don't smell the humus
I don't even smell the Tabbouleh
I don't smell the taxi's
I don't smell the mosque's ancient rug
As the shooting starts again,
I only smell fear

BEAUTY IN THE CRACKS
Wild Flower

I have no idea where I'm going but I will walk as far as my feet will carry me.

I'm looking over my shoulder now watching a timeline of memories condensed into the very shaping of my existence.

I stand for a moment allowing the warmth of my tears to fall off my chin. Not before they pass the smile I have waited so long to feel.

Every moment that meant anything to me is now safely stored.

I touch my heart and give a silent thanks.

Every scar, every fall, every hug, every uncontrollable laughing session, every worry, every breakthrough has molded me.

Beauty can be found in the darkest of lights. It's not always a sunset or a mountain or your first morning sip of coffee.

We grow and spread in so many directions always asking for the map, *the path of least resistance.*

I have found the bigger the struggle the more rewarding the end is. Eventually you realize what you cried about years ago you may smile about now.

Life is a journey.

Open your eyes, take it all in and breathe.

Perspectives will shift, people will grow and leave and maybe come back. Maybe not.

I see all colors of the spectrum and embrace the dullness of the grey.

I don't know where I'm going, but I will walk as far as my feet will carry me.

I will look back from time to time and I will remember my home.

I will cry, I will smile, and I will wish that you all find the beauty in cracks too.

ANGER
A Horrible Mistress
Ngang God'swill N.

Anger is a pushy mistress;
with a daring smile,
claws as needles
and a touch that ignites.

She breaks my heart,
my nature, my form, my deeds.
Given irrevocable strokes
to her ice cold laughter.

I am in her arms again;
her rage my courage.
Turning me from man to beast.

Her love is so unstable,
high, low, none-existent.
Inconsistent in existence,
born of a troubled heart.

Unlike her, I regret.
Because of her, I regret.
yet her presence is alluring,
a passion to make right.

Still, here I am
when her rage is gone,
her warm touch alien
my beating heart free again.

I face the courts alone,
the Karma that awaits,
consequences unfailing.

While she lies in wait, safe.

She is a backstabber,
like the beautiful Delilah,
though more deadly, so,
with a grip on the soul.

I find myself alone again.
How did I get here?
Where did my lover go,
with her fire and justifications?

She is reality, no doubt,
though not born as I am
but a child of my heart.

For all her crimes I must suffer.

A COLLECTION OF ECHOES
Marika Bianca

flames

I was a fire buried deep,
the smell of smoke
wafting from
an echo in the bone,
when you knowingly
took my hand
and fanned the flames

winter

How we reach
for the green of things from summers past
only to have them shatter
in icy winter's grasp.

leaving

for you are tired of
competing
with a memory

echoes

I heard echoes of
what might have been,
the taste of
broken promises
on my lips
like copper pennies,
as you pulled
my skirt up

PREVIDYA: TOUCH OF SUMMER
Garrett Copeland

Across a bed of winter snow, you snared
me.

You're smaller now but still tall~ less myth,
more real.

The priests would hate this, and you. You slide up to me, coal~
black lips and fingertips, with teeth too white to believe, and eyes
the color of my pounding heart. Your touch is warm and smooth
as a summer breeze against my throat, and I shudder. What
would a heathen god want with me?

Your chest is bare, and lean, but you're not cold. The split in your
kilt displays an expanse of black thigh and hints of a swell that
steals my breath. Your fingers trace the edge of my scalp, silver in
my skin, curve of my breast. Your touch sends shivers up my
spine. That smirk shines like the sun, and the drum in my chest
races faster.

The priests would have my head,
but…

Your lips tingle on my ear. Your breath's warm and you smell like
flowers, and musk, and magic. My knees knock together. My

insides coil into knots. My body moves. My lips find yours. My hands claw at your back, through your mane. My leg plunges through that kilt. A drum thunders in my ears and I have to feed this need.

What would a heathen god want with me? Who's to say.

The priests can pray, but I have a god~ if just for today.

THE SECRETS THE MOON HOLDS

Terrye Turpin

She ran along the path, a shortcut through the park near her home. The blue-white glow from the full moon the only illumination as she dodged through trees as familiar to her as the furniture in her living room.

She emerged from the woods onto the concrete sidewalk, a thirty-three year old woman still able, she felt, to pass as one much younger. Still happy for the inconvenience of being carded when she ordered wine, her mock indignation hiding her false pleasure.

The moon her only observer, she fussed with the zipper on her jacket and reached up to pull loose a strand from her ponytail. Messy enough to give the patina of truth to her exercise, the flushed cheeks and high color on her chest.

Home at last, she paused before she turned the knob and pushed open the door. If he greets her with a kiss, she wonders, will he taste him on her lips?

ROSA IMMORTAL

Phyllis Romero

Genesis.
Infinitesimal nucleus
scattered into the earth,
intumesce,
bursting.

Her ingénue beauty unveiled,
prickling thorns
sheltering
her wounded heart
as she rises.

Immortal,
see her rise,
arching for the heavens.
At last, *she reigns,*
enveloped by petals
soft as crimson velvet.

Resilient,
defiant as Mother Earth.
Rosettes, intoxicating the fields
with her sweet nectar,
caressed by Anemos,
unfolding her full beauty.

Once a fair maiden,
now a queen — Rosa.

Her soul dances,
swaying gently
in the breeze,
unshackled from the constraints
of her birthing.

TAOHUA CHUNTIAN

Randy Shingler

Fresh morning dew
Fragrant blossoms
Sun glistening air
Sensory aliveness
Peach Blossom Spring.

Winding river streams
Smooth gray stones
Verdant tree shoots
Yellow daffodils
Peach Blossom Spring.

Tree nestled arcade
Melodious song birds
Scattered daisy petals
Solitary garden pleasure
Peach Blossom Spring.

Winding river streams, flower strewn banks
Face curved smiles, distant mountain peaks
Utopian beauty, nature's harmonious presence,
Taohua Chuntian, Peach Blossom Spring.

A Chinese fable, **The Peach Blossom Spring (Taohua Chuntian)** was written during a time of political instability and national disunity. It was written by poet and scholar, Tao Yuanming in 421

CE.

It is about a fisherman who haphazardly wanders into a hidden utopian community filled with only blossoming peach trees and people contentedly hidden from society's instability. It has inspired many paintings, poems, plays and movies.

THE LUXE SUITE WITH A VIEW OF PARIS

Jean N.

Your window,
it has a beautiful view in shades of pink.

The glass is tinted dexterously.
A devious artist.
A master, work that should be artfully appreciated.

Look outside, I dare you.

Spot the Champs-Elysées with its aisles of symmetry,
snaking through the glorious streets of crisp, burnt leaves.
Not a shade of difference between right or left, right or wrong.

The sight of gold inlays materializing moment by moment.

It's enough to make a greedy man sated for a million equinoxes.
Look down and embrace the wonder that fills you,
that they, down below feel.
They seem to feel something, something real
don't they?

Do you see that man in that smart, smoke-colored suit?
He's striking in that uniform,
But he shouldn't be coveted.
Cover your eyes instead with your blanket of purity,
your nose, q u i c k
don't inhale his corruption,
don't asphyxiate yourself with your own futile envy.

He's weighed down by the burdens he carries in his lightweight
briefcase.

You don't see it?
That's alright, you can keep looking outside.
You're young,
Still enclosed in these walls of luxury; sanctity.

Your luxe suite — it has a beautiful view of Paris in Autumn.
But beware, the window has a rose tint;
everything is perfect.

      Step outside, I dare you.
      See the World as it really is.

ROADS

Showmock Ghosh

We are the roads that sweep into the horizon
Over the foggy hills and by the timeless oceans
The people we meet, are the milestones that pass us by,
The memories we make are the discarded cigarette stubs,
Tossed away once they have run out,
Reminders of the stolen moments
That our lives are made out of.

Like the summer rain that bears down incessantly on dusty roads, time continues to eat away at our hearts — stripping us off the memories that we had collected with every passing day of spring. Like the boxes that children draw on roads and hop across, dissolve with the rain. Until, like the roads, we are revealed in our state of vulnerability.

Until all that remain are the cavities in our souls that we had taught ourselves to forget, spaces we had filled up hurriedly with the dust of our skins.

THE TRUTH ABOUT LOVE
Nawekulo Wanjugu

1.
I'm hard to love
Correction,
I'm not easy to love:

When you approach me (because I'm too awkward to make the
first move) you'll be met by one of two responses, either an
awkward smile, or a surprised look and silence. All in all, one
factor is constant, the first encounter will be awkward.

2.
I'm hard to love,
Correction,
I'm not easy to love:

All corresponding meetings will vary in content. Some days I'll
take the comic route and attempt to be funny (kindly bear with
me), sometimes I'll take the philosophical route (again, kindly
bear with me) and sometimes, I'll be quiet (that's your cue to
either join me in silence, or feel free to speak).

3.
I'm hard to love,
Correction,
I'm not easy to love:

I don't cry in public. So, when you see me about to break, please
don't try to hug me, that'll just bring on the waterworks (another

awkward moment between us) and I am not the prettiest crier.

4.
I'm hard to love,
Correction,
I'm not easy to love:

Sometimes, I'll disappear, go incognito for a while. Do not fret, everything is okay. I usually need to detach myself from the world. A way of rebooting.

5.
I'm hard to love,
Correction,
I'm not easy to love:

I'm not very good at people…ing or talking about my emotions. Some of the words that may come out of my mouth, may come off as harsh or insensitive. I need you to understand that it's never my goal, I don't mean any harm, I'm just not very good at it.

6.
I am hard to love,
Correction,
I'm not easy to love:

I talk to myself, all the time. I'm currently holding two board meetings in my head. Sometimes, the people I'm conversing with want to take a stroll outside, this may be evident in the sudden flailing of arms or movement of the lips that you are sure to witness from me. Don't panic, the residents will soon go back to their respective homes.

7.
I am hard to love,
Correction,
I'm not easy to love:

I have trust issues. I have both attachment and detachment issues.
I'm not the clingy type, but I do love a good cuddle. I'll give you
your space.

8.
I am hard to love,
Correction,
I'm not easy to love:

I like fixing things (one of the interests my father passed on to
me). If a bulb needs to get changed, I'll do it, if something breaks,
I'll try to put it back together. I don't mind, I actually enjoy it. We
can fix things together.

9.
I am hard to love,
Correction,
I'm not easy to love:

My definition of masculinity, 'what makes you a man', may differ
from the norm.

What makes you a man is asking whether I'm okay, because you
are genuinely concerned or you listening to what I have to say
because you value my opinion. It's you opening up, especially
about the emotional stuff, telling me your hopes, your dreams,
and, most especially, your fears. Tell me what I did that hurt your
feelings.

It's you trying to calm me do down when I get overly excited, you
encouraging me to be a better human-being, and letting me do the
same for you, us, being able to have a mature conversation, even
when tempers are running high, because, trust me, when you're
with me, tempers will run high on numerous occasions.

It's you feeling comfortable and secure enough to ask for help when you need it and not being afraid to break down in front of me.

10.
I'm hard to love,
Correction,
I'm not easy to love,

but your heart will never find safer hands.

THE BEANIE BABY MURDER
Steve B. Howard

The green filth had grown over the grate and locked his memory away from this street. Homelessness was punishable by banishment from recognition. The law was enacted to make them forget his existence, but now he had pushed his way through the hidden sewers and stood before the gift shop, a representative of the rejected and abandoned.

He watched the motley horde of women fluttering around the display case as they cuddled the little stuffed toys like favored children. Leering at them through the opaque front window of the gift shop he felt the drool slip through the gap in his teeth and run down his chin. He was now free from the gutter society had supplied him with. *They are all beautiful compared to me,* he muttered aloud. His troll like exterior was reflected back to him in the window. Viewing his hunched backed body and one over-sized bulging eye in its socket caused him to cry in rage. *So unfair that I suffer while they browse.* He ran his hand through his three dozen long strands of muck covered hair as the tears ran down his pock marked moon crater cheeks.

The aristocratic wives and daughters did not notice his scared mass of damaged flesh weeping on the sidewalk. His pathetic figure did not reflect into their world. They shopped on oblivious to this suffering product of their husbands and fathers economic battles. To them he was only an abstraction; a disturbing news article scanned quickly and forgotten.

Opening his mouth, he stroked his large jutting front teeth and then moved his grimy fingers over his sharp canine teeth. The four remaining teeth on the top row were a great source of pride, but his favorite tooth was the serrated half nub that resided alone on the bottom row.

My teeth will grind, and they will respect. Their petty expenditures will not last another hour. He entered the gift shop grinding his teeth in preparation for his protest. He lurched proudly towards the large Beanie Baby display. With some difficulty he reached out with a shriveled hand and snatched up the cutest large eyed bundle of fur and fluff he could find. *This bit of triviality is the source of my suffering,* he thought staring down at the artificial cherub.

He had to gain the attention of the entire perfumed flock. Only by disturbing their world would they recognize his existence. He wailed out a long low scream, reproducing for a moment the cry of the hungry through out the store. The trampling conversations came to a halt and the fruity perfume rushed away from the brimstone odor wafting from his mouth. *I have the stupid butterflies attention now,* he thought. And it was true. Slowly his broken body with its yellow infected wounds and festering boils appeared amongst the tightly organized shelves full of expensive uselessness.

He held up the cute little chunk of fur and fluff so all the rainbow attired mall geese could get a good look at it's child like staring eyes. Then without hesitation he bit the head of the cute little Beanie Baby grinding the innocent eyes with his serrated half nub. The crowd of mall geese let loose a collective gasp as if he'd just chewed of the head of an adorable kitten.

Sitting behind her perch of authority, a rotund cashier wearing sharp glasses began to berate him with her tired monologue. *Sir, you'll have to pay for that, sir you have to pay for that item, sir you need to pay for that.*

Responding to her bland ramblings, a profane thought rose to the surface of his brain. *Pay for this indeed, my currency will be in the awareness I create.* But something went wrong when he attempted to utter his terrible answer. A hacking cough more grotesque than his ravaged body surprised him. Fur and white stuffing laced with black plastic and bloody teeth sprayed from his mouth.

Now enraged, he tried in vain to scream out his speech, but the Beanie Babies odd shaped head had embedded itself firmly in his throat. He turned red, then blue, then the green of death and money, finally collapsing to the ground in a twisted ball of ugly fatal twitches. The mall geese turned their collective attention back to buying pricey birthday presents, anniversary gifts, or simply wasting money. Having been trained not to understand, the bored cashier droned on, *Sir, you have to pay for that, sir you have to pay for that, sir…*

UBIQUITY
Creativivian

I saw dust dancing around my fingers
suspended gold,
absence mirroring absence.

I listened to dust dancing around my fingers
mute and talkative,
spoons full of ancient wars
now replaced by silence.

I sliced time and space into
thick coordinates,
to be here
and somewhere else,
to dip my feet into the mud of now
and somewhen else.

I am something different
than the sum of my arts.

BURNED

Jackie Ann

My heart trembled
under his hand
I wanted to be
whatever he wanted
But who was I
after that?

When he decided
I wasn't worth it,
who did I become?
After I melted in his mold
the world could not hold me
anymore

If my timid touch was not enough
I'm sorry
Why couldn't he give me a chance
to bloom
instead of digging up my roots
and leaving me naked
in the wilderness

Was I worth that little to him?
Did he have to crush
my outstretched arms,
disregard my womanhood?

I cannot trust myself to love

When I should have been grateful
for his absence
I pulled his shadow closer
so as not to lose him completely

I held on to the senseless dream of him
until the sun burned it out

And this is how the stars help you

SEVEN COLORS OF HOME
LB

The evening light peaked through the caves in the clouds, and spilled steadily across the hillside. We walked until we could see it radiating over the riverbanks… where we spent our summers, swimming as kids.

It emitted a familiar warmth that was strongest right after a long stretch of rain. *The moment felt full, as we were immersed in a shared state of renewal.* We felt our bodies pause and reunite with our lifeline.

A calm and soulful reminder washed over us. This would always be our home… a carved out, special place that for so long was the only world we knew. The sun was like our family, and had always been right there with us.

My mother once explained to us that the sun was made up of seven colors, for the seven of us kids, all from different families and backgrounds. We were Violet, Indigo, Blue, Green, Yellow, Orange, and Red. I used to think about that, right before we tumbled down the grassy hills… toppling into each other, *in our own scattered light spectrum.*

Smiling, we would all lay on the grass, catching our breath… until we settled into one color, glowing under the setting sun.

BRAND NAME

Elizabeth Helmich

I've decided to be French,
Now I don't have to care
About anything that goes
Into my mouth, only no excess,
That's the secret key to success!

Now that I'm French
My purchases — fresh, bright things,
Accessories make a lady, you know
If I become permanent bling, a gold rush
Entrance in lamé, apropos

It's easy, when you're French,
A path will greet me when I take
The next step, lively out a painted door,
My needs to be met, just as soon
As I choose to give the world — *more!*

Since I'm an all-new me,
My high heels match my highlights,
A smile lightbulbs my whole day,
Faking it until making it
Only works when we fail to play

I'm really not French,
Still the very same old me,
Learning how to *be*, more
Than an inner plea, my outer
Surface reflecting all that *I* see

Hello there, how do you do?
I'd really enjoy a glimpse
Of a less faulty point of view,
The pleasure's all mine, truly,
To meet, to greet…*you.*

I DON'T WANT TO SLEEP

Agnes Louis

Underneath the ink sky.
The stars spilling off the edge of heaven.
The cool summer breeze gently brushed my skin.
I don't want to sleep.

The ocean sang.
The waves whispered from the darkness.
Beckoning,
Come closer.

Your voice,
intertwined with mine.
Our laughter echoed,
in the space between our breaths.

My fingers in yours.
I closed my eyes and I heard.
The waves lapping on the white sand,
breaking at the shore.

I opened my eyes and I could see,
feel — your smile.

In your eyes,
I saw the twinkling stars,
magnificent dreams.

A whole new world,
a self-made reality.

Ready to be realized,
to be occupied.

No.
I don't want to sleep.

I could sit there forever.
I could look at you,
listen to you forever.
And I couldn't help but think,

I don't want to sleep,
just yet.

MY MOMMA'S CURSE

Tam Jackson

There are some things that you need to know about me. Things that affect you. So, listen. When my momma was about five years old, her momma up and left her. Yep, my grandma excused herself from the breakfast table one fine country morning and walked right out the front door. Then, she just drove off and left her drinking, farming husband and their four little kids. Like she never even knew 'em. My grandma was cursed, you see. Before she ran off, she passed that curse on to my momma. Now, I'm not saying that she passed it to her on purpose. I'm just saying that's what mommas can do if they aren't careful: they can pass on a curse that was passed on to them. Without even knowing it, sometimes without even being around to watch the curse mutate and grow and destroy, that's just what mommas can do.

It was the 1940s, and hell, not a whole bunch of women walked out on their kids back then. It was a mighty stressful time, though. The Great Depression had just ended, and our country was smack-dab in the middle of World War II. Women didn't have a lot of options. There was no such thing as effective birth control; women often had a whole mess of little ones before the ripe old age of 25. My grandma was tired of being tired, I guess. She couldn't deal with cotton fields and cotton diapers, anymore. Now, you might be tempted to believe that she tried to take my momma with her when she left, but that's not so. The truth is that she flat-out didn't want my momma. She didn't want her at all. The problem was, neither did anybody else.

My momma was *"given"* to her aunt. That's how they talk about it. Like my great-aunt won a pie at a carnival. *"Here, it's all yours!"* While I'd like to believe that this tough old broad who agreed to take my momma in had some semblance of love hidden way down deep in her big ole' bones, she sure never saw fit to share any love with my momma. No, sir. My momma was just her field hand; she was her hired help. In exchange for room and board, my momma managed cows and pigs and chickens and tomatoes and okra and such. She wasn't family; she was living, breathing **PROPERTY**. And she damn well knew it.

She was a cursed little girl. She grew up fast, and she grew up physically strong. But like most kids who get a great big punch in the heart so young, my momma never REALLY grew up. She stayed emotionally STUCK right there at age five, the age when her momma abandoned her. Even when my momma passed from this earth at the chronological age of 79, she was still just a lost and lonely five-year-old girl, forever waiting for her momma to come back and tell her that she was worth loving.

Just like her daddy had done before her, my momma fell into drinking. Yeah, she fell hard into that sorrow. My poor, sad, drunken momma often ended up letting poor, sad, drunken men crawl into bed with her. If they told her that she was pretty (which she was but didn't know it), they could slip her slip off, take a little slice of her soul, and then drive off like they never even knew her. She watched a lot of men drive off over the years. That was her momma leaving her and never looking back right there. Each time. Over and over. That was her curse. She wasn't worth gettin' to know or stickin' around for. At least, that's how she saw it.

In her futile attempts to fight off this curse, my momma shuffled men in and out of her life, one after another. After another. Each damaging and disappointing encounter confirmed to her that she was (just as she had always suspected) unworthy of respect or love — that she was, indeed, cursed. And just like her momma had done before her, my momma had a bunch of babies early in life. I was the second of her four *"Uh-Oh! What am I gonna do now?"* kids. And, dammit, we ALL inherited that evil curse: the curse of never feeling good about taking up space on this earth, never feeling wanted or loved or of any value at all.

I've spent my whole life trying to outrun that curse. Lord

knows I didn't always run fast enough. But I determined THIS after all those years of running: I won't pass that curse along to you. It stops HERE. With me. Because I choose to fight. For my children, for both of you, I choose to fight. I renounce this self-fulfilling prophecy; I defy this destiny of doom. I reject this wicked inheritance of self-loathing and self-sabotage.

I choose NOT to walk around with a hole in my heart. I won't be forever seeking to fill that hole with bad relationships, with drugs, with destructive behaviors that make me feel better for an instant — but then make the hole bigger. And bigger. And BIGGER. Until that hole grows into a massive, swirling vortex of pain that is forever sucking in more, more, and even MORE pain. Until that pain imprisons me, paralyzes me with its constant confirmation of my overwhelming **NOTHINGness**.

I choose to fight this miserable fate. For now, for always and forever, I choose to fight. And by making that one choice, that one shamelessly defiant, audacious choice, all my other choices become apparent. I choose to counter the voices in my head that were taught to me by the voices in my mother's head that were taught to her by the voices in her mother's head. They whisper, *"You are ugly. You are worthless. You are nothing. Never forget that, little girl.* **You. Are. NOTHING.***"* Those voices haunt me if I let them. So, I choose to quit letting them.

I choose to be physically healthy. I choose NOT to be a drunken victim of circumstance, a doped-up rendition of the women in my family that suffered before me. I choose NOT to put a needle into my arm and slink down to the ground in a slow suicide of resignation. I choose to be emotionally healthy; I choose to surround myself with people that value, respect and affirm me. I choose NOT to let another human being define me, dominate me, or destroy me. I choose to be thankful; I choose to wake up each day in exuberant anticipation of the sunrise, and I choose to go to sleep each night with an ardent appreciation for one more sunset.

I choose to be content. I never once got to see my momma content; not once in all her life was she ever at peace. But I'm not gonna live that way. I choose to be content. And, most of all, I choose to love; I choose to both give and receive abundant, spectacular, healing love.

So, hear me, my children. Listen. I had a beautiful, very sad momma. And she had a beautiful, very sad momma, and before them, there were so, so many beautiful, sad mommas in this family. It's been a curse for generation after generation — for as long back as anyone can remember. But, I've broken it now. You are free. Because I am a WARRIOR. Because I choose to fight. For you, my children. Every damn glorious day, and with all that is in me, I choose to fight.

I love you,
Momma

MOJOJORN
Angie Granheim

I think of you when I see the evergreens
I don't know why they remind me of you,
maybe its because it feels like Minnesota,
and Minnesota goes hand in hand with you.

Similar, two of a kind in many ways,
both of us in places we don't really belong.
Content in our discomfort,
invisible in our lives,
we make ourselves seen somehow.
Intentional attention in the form of a snap.
Bubbles and bath tubs,
nails down backs.

Mojo brings a smile whenever it appears.
Maybe things would be different,
if we could go back in time a few years.
But here we are,
from time to time we talk,
we snap,
we chat.
But always know that you cross my mind,
whenever the wind blows,
and the smell of the Evergreens rise up,
and remind me of you.

LAY WITH ME
(Interlude III)
Walker Jo Lee

lay with me,
in trust
harmony
soft island
peace
memories and silence.

lay with me,
don't tread my dreams
of simple revolution
of personal evolution.
dry clouds,
settling the black sea.

lay with me,
earth shakes
flooded heart
split atoms
i have to save me
for myself

lay with me,
don't cover my voice.
i have to keep pieces
of me, to myself
to know all the beauty
i can be,
when you're away.

NIGHT CREATURES

T.S. Narkissa Luna

Steeped in old poetry,
Languished delicate harpies,
Each,
With a different story.

But ghost or not,
They live in my body,
My bed,
And convicted memories.

Criminal at best,
When surrounded by satires,
Legends of foggies without testimony,
Only proverbial crowned crowds for the witnessing.

Thickly or not,
Memorable or not,
They own the corridors,
As they waved authority.

Their bonds drenched in regrets,
Unforgotten blisters,
Crimson mirrors in the halls,
Their nails clinging to my mind.

Creatures of the night,
Honing in their spite,
Dreamers in their hearts,

And choices held tight.

Women and men,
Of my past still,
Hold me,
I'm fighting to cut their cords.

My bones creak and crack with wires,
A fight to the morrow,
A break of myself —
Impossible.

A CATALOG OF QUIET, BURNING THINGS

Guérin Asante

The better nature of our blooming angel's trumpet:
three feet deep, and breezes, and manure,
cracked against the dry concrete nearby, while
we are writing in a catalog of quiet, burning things
whose warmth we can never truly feel, only hint to,
in the sting our shovels pour into our muscles,
while liquid crystals dot our skin — some of them returning
stars, like faultless tears descending our brows
back into our eyes.

DUSKY RAINDROPS
Dennett

Dusky raindrops
Heralding twilight,
Whispering faintly
To shadowy creatures
In shrouded places,

Come forth, come forth,
Your time is now.

A NEW FRIEND FOR DARIUS

Shea Oliver

"Do you have any questions about your son's prescriptions for Chlorpromazine or Prozac?" asked the pharmacist.

"No, his psychiatrist explained to me what I needed to know," the well-dressed woman replied without even a glance at the teenager by her side, "Theodore will take them as prescribed."

Theodore looked at his mother as she paid for the drugs. He knew the pills wouldn't make any difference. Darius wasn't in his imagination.

The drive home was even duller than the appointment with the head shrink.

"I don't want to take those drugs," stated the teen, as much to himself as to the woman driving the overpriced station wagon with the ostentatious hood ornament.

"Doesn't matter, you need them," rebuked Mother, "You're a teenager now, and it's past time to be done with imaginary friends."

"I don't have imaginary friends. Darius is real."

"That's enough of this conversation. If you can't be rational, at least be quiet."

Theodore watched as the mature oak and maple trees zipped past in a blur, partially obscuring the stone and timber houses set behind iron fences in his neighborhood. He wondered how many of the other homes contained someone like Darius hiding in their dark spaces.

Mother punched the code into the keypad, and the iron gate creaked loudly on its hinges as their vehicle idled in the long driveway. Theodore sighed knowing that it was nothing more than false security for a home filled with insecurity and danger.

She parked the car on the curved path sweeping its way to the front door. Theodore opened the car's backdoor and stepped into the dreary mist that clung damply to everything that it touched.

"I'll be back before bedtime," his mother said expecting and receiving no response, "take one of each of those pills when you get inside." She drove away, leaving Theodore shivering by himself at the front door.

While adults always proclaimed their admiration whenever they first stepped into the house, Theodore didn't share their feelings about the structure. It was big and old with its own dark, lonely personality. The stairs creaked, even without someone stepping on them. The antique paintings watched everything with eyes devoid of emotion. Cold air brushed across your face and slid down your shirt, even while standing in front of the great room's gigantic, roaring fireplace.

Theodore closed the heavy oak door aggressively behind himself, and the ornate brass knocker clanked against its strike plate outside.

"I'm home," he shouted into the dimly light entryway, knowing that he was the only living soul in the house. The silence screamed back, but he ignored its endless empty reply.

He walked to the back of the house and kicked his shoes into the mudroom by the backdoor. Glancing back at the way he came, he saw the wet, dirty tracks of each of his steps on the polished wood floor.

"Shit," he said, realizing he should have taken the shoes off before he came through the house, "Oh well, she'll be pissed no matter what I do."

The pills slid down his throat easily as he gulped the last bit of milk in the jug. Rummaging through the refrigerator, he found some lunch meat and cheese for a sandwich.

"Another glorious family dinner," he announced as he sat alone at the long dining room table. He left the plate to remind the empty house that once again he ate alone, even though he knew it didn't care. The only thing that really paid him any attention here was Darius.

The cloudy sunset cast an orange tint on the well-manicured backyard and lake stretching behind their property. Theodore stood barefoot on the old bricks in the sunroom. They felt warm on his feet after the sun heated the red blocks of clay during the day. With so many cold things in this house, the momentary heat warmed his feet, but he knew that it wouldn't last.

His eyes followed the path of lights around the lake to 842 Oakstead Drive, Mr. Charles Patterson's estate on the far side of the lake. His mansion was even more pretentious than Theodore's family's extravagant house.

He knew that in that mansion is where his mother would be — pretending that the other parts of her life didn't exist. Father would stay at his apartment in the city, blindly assuming that mother would care for the child.

They both excelled only at caring for themselves.

Darius told him once that his loneliness called the boy out from the darkness, but Theodore believed that his anger called Darius too. Darius never refuted his supposition. He simply smiled with a coldness that only death itself can paint.

"Pills?" giggled Darius nefariously as the sun succumbed to the shroud of the night. Its blackness wrapping the world in secrecy and shadows.

Theodore held his gaze on the ripples of light reflecting on the lake from the stubby light posts tracing their way in an endless circle around the water.

"She thinks that pills will whisk me away?" laughed Darius coldly from someplace behind Theodore, "You can't hope me away. You can't think me away."

"I know," replied Theodore. He turned and looked around the room. The glass windows covering three walls reflected Theodore's image and all of the furniture and decorations of the room, but nothing else revealed itself in the dark panes.

The baseball bashed into the back of Theodore's head.

"Play ball," announced Darius as Theodore scanned for signs of where Darius might be hiding.

"Not tonight. I have too much on my mind."

"Are you hoping that the pills will make me go away?"

"I know they won't," replied Theodore crassly, "Nothing makes you go away."

The boy's callous laughter disappeared down the hallway towards the kitchen. Theodore followed the sound into the long room featuring a wide, open fireplace for cooking. The room begged for a redesign but only suffered the misplacement of modern appliances.

"Goddamnit, Darius," cursed Theodore as he began replacing the scattered orange pills and green capsules into their bottles, "What the hell do you want?"

"To play," replied Darius, "You're my only friend, and I want to play."

"Maybe later," said Theodore to the empty space where the boy's voice emanated.

When all the pills were back in their bottles, Theodore padded his way up two flights of stairs, walked solemnly down the hallway, and opened the door to another staircase. Moonlight streamed in through the windows wrapping the large office situated higher than any other part of the house.

Father's big telescope hogged the space in front of the windows facing the lake. Theodore pointed the large tube toward the back of 842 Oakstead Drive.

"She's there again, isn't she?" asked Darius.

"Of course," retorted Theodore, "She'd rather be with him than her family."

"You know the solution."

"Fuck off, Darius," snapped the annoyed teenager as he looked around the room, hoping to catch a glimpse of the boy who tormented him every night.

"I want to play," demanded the boy with anger swelling in his tone, "I want to play, now. I don't want to wait until later."

"Okay, stop," snapped Theodore as he felt the sharp pressure on his arm, "I'll check the traps. Just give me a fucking minute, you little bastard."

Theodore's toes mushed into the wet mulch of the garden.

The heavy mist turned to rain as his flashlight beam revealed the hissing rat trapped in the cage behind the evergreen bush. The rodent screeched obscenities as its wire prison cell was roughly carried into the house.

Even before Theodore opened the door to go back into the mudroom, he could hear Darius' menacing giggle bouncing off the wainscoted walls.

Theodore set the trap on the floor in the mudroom, opened the pest's cage, and the rat charged out. The rodent ran less than five paces before its head and neck smashed against the floor. The small creature snarled and hissed as its floated upward in the air with its neck and torso smushed as if someone was gripping it tightly.

The crunch of bone followed by sucking and slurping sounds signaled that Darius' meal met with his satisfaction.

Theodore watched as the blood left the rodent and appeared to float in the air while the dying sacrificial offering deflated like a helium balloon after too many days. Another chomp and sloppy gulping sound followed as Darius' greedy face appeared with his teeth clamped hard on the rat's neck and shoulder. His eyes ablaze and flushed red with blood.

Theodore watched in horrific, mesmerized silence. Each greedy draw of the rat's blood into Darius' mouth flowed away from his pointy teeth, filling in more parts of the child's body. No matter how many times he witnessed the ghost child take human form, Theodore shuddered at the thought of what the little hell-spawned boy really wanted.

"Thank you, big brother," piped Darius as his arms wrapped around Theodore, hugging him tightly, "You're the best."

Theodore studied the boy's hair against his chest. Every dark strand perfectly combed. The boy's black suit, white shirt, and dark red tie remained neatly pressed. Night after night, the boy's attire looked exactly as it had while the child rested in the open coffin that his parents presented in the great room to mourning family and grandiloquent guests.

But the Darius that Theodore remembered didn't have this

pale skin that shimmered with a ghostly radiance. Its translucence glowed of its own accord, even in the absence of light. While the boy's skin was disquieting, the child's glowing red eyes pressed any sympathy for his brother to the back corners of Theodore's mind.

As much as he wanted to be repulsed and push the child away, he hugged Darius back as he grappled with the guilt of not protecting his little brother better. He could feel the bump and disconnected vertebrae in the boy's back where the boy landed against the table when Father threw him in anger.

Darius stepped back from Theodore and announced, "It's time to play."

The brothers launched into the same nightly ritual that many siblings share. A ball tossed back and forth. Cars racing down long hallways. Wrestling and laughing without another care in the world.

"Darius, I have to go bed soon," said Theodore when a recess in their antics gave him pause him to glance at the clock.

"When will you finally help me?" inquired the boy.

"I don't know," replied Theodore, "Soon, maybe, I don't know."

The red tint in Darius' eyes glowed brighter and darker as he listened to his brother's response. The car in the boy's hand flew across the room, smashing into a thousand pieces against the wall.

"I see the gash across your face," screamed the angry child, "She hit you again; she's making you take those pills. How long do you have, brother, before you join me?"

Theodore ran the tips of his fingers across the long wound on his cheek. Mother's ring dug a trench that morning when she struck him as he lay in bed.

"But Darius did it!" he'd protested at her as he felt the warm blood oozing through his fingers while pressing them hard against his face.

"Not another word from you," she'd yelled angrily at the teen as he tried to get out of bed, "Put every one of these fucking toys and clothes back where they belong!"

Theodore's eyes pleaded with his little brother to find a different solution, to map a variant outcome, but Darius glared back at Theodore. As much as he didn't want to, he accepted that the little dead boy understood the adult occupants of this house as well as anyone.

"Join me or bring her to me," stated the angry child, "I need someone to play with me."

Theodore stared at his ghostly little brother. The knot in his stomach grew tighter and tighter. Anger, pity, and confusion slushed through his gut. He knew in his heart that the demon child was right. One day he would join the boy if he didn't help the child soon.

"Okay," Theodore said, relinquished, "But how do you know that she'll come?"

"Do what I told you to do, I promise that the little girl at 842 Oakstead Drive wants to have a friend as badly as I do," said Darius, the angry red tint in his eyes moderating. The little boy looked at his feet for a moment and then stared back at his older brother, "It's lonely here and I just, I just want a friend to play with me."

Theodore counted out a handful of white sleeping tablets from the bottle in Mother's medicine cabinet and walked back to the kitchen. After grinding them into a fine powder with the mortar and pedestal from the pantry, he carefully poured the dust into the half-empty bottle of wine in the refrigerator. He spun the bottle by the neck until he couldn't see any remains or residue floating in the dark liquid.

Theodore and Darius hid when they heard the door to the mudroom open.

"Goddamn, that child," barked Mother as she slammed the door closed and began marching toward the kitchen, "Another bloody mess in the mudroom, tracks on my wood floor, and plates left on my dining room kitchen. Why did I ever bother having children?"

The pair watched the refrigerator open and close from the

shadows. Darius stifled a giggle as Mother passed near them on her way upstairs with a wine glass in her hand, the burgundy liquid reaching nearly to the brim.

"Mother?" inquired Theodore loudly into the moon-lit master bedroom after some time had passed. The pace of her quiet snoring notched up and faded back down as the only response she could give.

In the kitchen, Darius handed the phone receiver to Theodore. "He won't answer," stated the little boy flatly, "Just leave a message."

Theodore rotated the finger wheel repeatedly and waited. The tell-tell click of an answering machine answered with Father's recorded voice.

"Father! This is Theodore. Come home quick! It's terrible! You have to get here fast!" exclaimed the teen into the phone, quickly hanging it up.

Darius snickered and punched his brother's arm.

"Okay, Darius," exhaled Theodore, "I guess there's no turning back now."

Theodore walked quickly in the cold night air, following the path illuminated by the stubby light posts wrapping themselves around the dark lake.

Moss caked the old stones sinking into the ground, protecting the open stairway leading down to the cellar entrance at 842 Oakstead Drive.

Theodore pushed his finger along the top of the bottom row of stones, finding a wide groove filled with dirt. Using his fingernail, he clawed out the little opening, and a key clattered as bounced onto the landing in front of the cellar door.

"Damn," muttered Theodore as he picked up the key and fitted it into the door's lock, "That little demon bastard was right."

Carefully closing the door behind him, Theodore paused to turn on his flashlight, its weak battery barely illuminating the space around his feet. The girlish giggle from the shadows stiffened his spine.

"You came for me?" the quiet, young voice whispered from the darkness.

Theodore pointed the light in the direction of the sound, but only found the remnants of long-forgotten junk.

"I guess so," he replied when his nerves finally began to steel themselves for the task at hand, "I think you're supposed to follow me."

Theodore carefully navigated to the stairs and exited the musty confines of the basement to find himself in a hallway that led to the great room. Charles Patterson snored loudly with an arm and a leg hanging off the couch. He hadn't moved since Theodore spotted him through the telescope in Father's office. The empty glass on the coffee table butted against the empty bottle of scotch.

He slipped the flashlight into his pocket and wrapped both hands around the baseball bat's handle. Stepping behind the couch, he yelled, "Patterson, wake up!"

The groggy man snapped upright, baffled by the noise. Before he could react, Theodore swung the wooden bat as hard as he could at the back of the man's head. The cracking sound bounced off the large floor-to-ceiling windows overlooking the lake, and Mr. Patterson's body crumbled to the ground like a discarded tissue.

"Oh my, oh my," the tiny female voice proclaimed, "What on earth have you done?"

The broken bat clattered as Theodore weakly tossed it across the room. Sitting down on the couch, he pressed his hands together in a vain attempt to stop their shaking. He looked away from the body sprawled on the floor and forced his eyes closed. Opening them back up, he knew it wasn't a nightmare, or at least it wasn't the type of nightmare that you have while sleeping.

Steadying his breathing, he bent down and pulled Mr. Patterson's belt off and then wrapped it around both of the man's ankles, cinching it tightly.

"This is your ride," Theodore spoke into the darkness, "I don't know how, but I guess you can get inside him."

The girlish giggle grew closer and closer, and the man groaned as if he'd been hit by the bat again.

"Girl, are you in there?"

Another strained grunt and moan emanated from Mr. Patterson. Theodore looked closely at the man's face, and its features were contorted and disfigured.

"I guess you are," winced Theodore grabbing the belt and pulling the man toward the side door of the mansion. He pocketed the keys to the man's overpriced German sedan from the hook by the door and pulled the man out into the driveway.

Sweat beaded on his head as he hauled Mr. Patterson's unconscious body into the back seat of the car. The man groaned with each tug but remained trapped in the forced slumber caused by the blow to his head.

The engine roared to life, and Theodore gripped the leather-wrapped steering wheel, driving up to the gate. He marvelled as it began to open without any action on his part.

The car keys jangled in his pocket as he fumbled to open the garage door back at his house on the other side of the lake. The smell of dirt and fertilizer assaulted his nose when he opened the door. Mother loved a pristine yard more than a protected car, so the gardener had the entire four-car garage at his disposal. Theodore quickly found the dolly and wheeled it to the car.

Mr. Patterson's head thunked hard on the concrete despite Theodore's best effort not to drop the body.

"Fuck," he cursed, "Son of a bitch is heavy."

The body barely fit on the dolly that the gardener used for moving heavy pots, but Theodore scavenged some rope from the garage and lashed Mr. Patterson tightly to it

Darius stood waiting at the door into the mudroom, dancing a little as Theodore rolled the dolly up the stairs and into the house. When they reached the staircase, Darius helped by pushing the dolly up while Theodore pulled.

Once Mr. Patterson's knees were snug with Father's side of the bed, Theodore untied the ropes, and the unconscious man flopped onto the bed next to their snoring Mother.

The boys heard the door to the mudroom slam, and they hurried into the closet, hiding the dolly, and leaving the door ajar so that they could see.

"What the ever living fuck?" demanded Father quietly as he looked at the two bodies lying in his bed, "Should have known what that bitch would do."

Father walked to the dresser and opened the bottom drawer, removing his revolver and a box of bullets. He glared at the bed, his breathing coming in angry snorts as he chambered six bullets. The click of the cylinder elicited a faint moan from Mother.

Theodore watched, unable to think as Father stood at the foot of the bed pointing the gun at each of them, seemingly indecisive about who would feel the wrath of his anger first. The barrel stopped moving as he lined it up with Mr. Patterson's chest. His wife bolted upright screaming as two quickly fired shots ripped into the unconscious man's chest.

Mother screamed as Father swung the weapon, pointing it at her.

The projectile bore a hole through her forehead, and blood splattered against the wall behind her. Mother fell back, her eyes looking toward the heaven she didn't deserve to see.

The boys watched as Father stood staring at the dead bodies. Despite his overwhelming desire to vomit and run, Theodore held his brother's arm to ensure that the child didn't rashly bolt into the room.

Father tossed the gun into the bottom drawer and turned back around to spew obscenities at the adulterous couple in his bed.

"And now, what the hell am I supposed to do with that other worthless child that you bore?" inquired Father as his rage diminished, "Two pathetic offspring, neither worth a stinking pile of shit."

Darius ripped his arm from Theodore's grip and quickly tiptoed to the dresser, removing the gun from where it landed.

"Hello, Father," said Darius leveling the revolver at the man, "did you miss me?"

"No, No, No! What the fuck?" stammered Father, spinning around with his face painted with fear upon seeing the apparition of his dead son, "You can't be real. What the hell is going on here?"

Theodore stepped out of the closet and looked at the confused and terrified man standing at the foot of the bed. Father's face reflected his inability to comprehend how the vision of the child that he'd killed stood before him. Sympathy might be warranted, but Theodore couldn't find anything but disappointment and resentment.

"Hehehehe, I'm free!" giggled a young girl's voice as the lamp on Father's nightstand crashed to the floor, "Darius, I'm finally here!"

Father's head spun around, scanning the room to locate another child, but he could only see two boys. The man's jaw clenched tightly, and he snorted at the boys, "What game are you little monsters playing?"

Darius tilted his head toward his older brother, his eyes red with fury and face erupting in a villainous smile. Theodore nodded affirmatively to the ghastly little boy holding the revolver.

Father buckled to the ground as the bullet smashed through his kneecap. His fall and scream shook the room, "You fucking nightmares!"

Darius walked closer to Father as the infuriated man attempted to push himself towards the bathroom and away from the demonic creature holding the gun. The boy pointed the revolver's barrel directly at Father's head, "My nightmare started when you killed me, yours will start today."

"No, no, no, please don't," begged Father, his tone changing with the realization of the danger that he was in, "Have mercy, I beg you."

A cruel grin spread across Darius' lips, and he giggled while he responded, "Okay Father, but now it's time to play."

Theodore watched the bite marks appear on Father's neck and the blood spurting out into the materializing mouth of the little girl. He sighed heavily, leaving the gruesome scene and heading down the stairs.

Huge raindrops poured down fiercely, beating against everything in waves outside the house. The water felt clean, pelting against his head when he stepped out of his home for the very last time.

"Theodore," came the little boy's voice from behind him.

"Yes, Darius?" he replied, turning around and letting the water drip down his face rather than return to the house.

"Thank you," said the little boy sheepishly, "You're the best brother ever."

For a moment, the boy's eyes seemed to turn green and morph back to the innocent eyes of a child. Theodore looked into those eyes, hoping to see the Darius that he loved and remembered so well.

A nearby strike of lightning lit up the sky, electrifying the air, and Theodore flinched, clamping his eyes closed in fright. When he looked back towards the door, Darius' eyes blazed deep red, and a malevolent smile dominated his face.

"Goodbye, Darius," Theodore said with a hint of sadness. It was his brother, but it wasn't his brother.

The engine of the German sedan roared to life again, and Theodore drove to the end of the driveway. He looked back into the house through the large bay window, shrugging and sighing as two small children jumped on the sofa in the front room.

"Have fun playing with your new friend," he said out loud, turning out of the driveway and accelerating as quickly as the car would go.

IAMBIC CHAOTIC

Lisa Sellge

spaceships, blueberries, and long spring grass
(once i had a lover)
cactus, coyotes, and heat
(fire would flicker through the blood in his hands)
levitation and sudden retreat
(and in his palace i could barely stand)
a soul with a sail and a beat
(and he was the light through a crack on the floor)
spirit blown cold in his sleep
(the shape of his kiss stained the back of my door)
salt smoke and bittersweet
(alone in the season of searching for more),
my gypsy and glass in the street.

IN ANOTHER LIFE
Existence

oxygen will cease to exist
when they, at last, hearken to our shrieks,
the frenzied screeches from the disparate rooms lenify,
reconstructing to murmurs of admiration
cleaving on to a speck of emotion,
a minor would adore the world,
just like the boy she attempted to seize the regard of.

The stars, would be espied as greater than
merely a base for our poetry
and would be esteemed by even the
men who do not heed their wives.

Words would be hindered from being exploited using a weapon
and altered into something alluring, life
we would deprive loneliness from unhinging us by dashing to
open arms,

instead of, to the pages that are drained from bearing the weight,
pushed upon the thin spaces,
words on the tips of our tongues shall flow out naturally
the require to exhort them diminishing.

We shall fortify each other from stumbling into the devilish
concrete floor,
rather than posting up the other direction so we would not

descend ourselves,
women would betake themselves to one another proffering their
innocence, not the bruits of the neighbors
the trees would possess a finer excuse for rendering us oxygen,
as opposed to feeling wroth with themselves
for granting us life,

the flowers would deem themselves as blessed when gleaned,
instead of wilting,
due to their supposed ill-fate.

The sleeping pills would be proven inutile to our needs,
and rather each soul would be clasped to another to remain
asleep,
per case, the entire world would come to be blind
and the beauteous ones would too be us,

for exceptional features would then yearn to serve a purpose.

I would not flinch staring them down,
unimportant how execrable the pain inflicted by them might be,
because I'll have nil to lose,

bitterly, the world abides as it is
mayhap when the water and sky call truce,
I'll perceive myself in heaven
that as of now is so far from becoming.

FREQUENCY

Giovanni Sonier

Undulating waves
crashed violently
against the rocky shores,
smoothing the once jagged
and blemished sediments,
beaches fully doused
by now ebbing tides;
the *Sea* withdrawing her grasp
from a lover beyond reach,
every day,
she nurtured the rich soil
for a *Herculean* tree that stood
deeply rooted in the Earth,
flaunting more lush hues
than the eye could capture,
he prevailed over thunderous winds,
his golden leaves and silvery bark glittering
on a forlorn hilltop that overlooked
the yawning cyanic expanse,
the expanse that he deeply admired,
the expanse that he longed to trace,
the expanse that his *veins* desired,
blue and green attracting one another;
the two mutually entangled,
yet never touching lips.

AT EASE
Fierce Force

At ease
If you please
I get my head on straight
Before it's too late
I was all in
Right out of the gate
A 16 month run
Epic and fun
Que the sudden change
Consuming toxic pain
Driving me insane
Not understanding the deal
And praying to heal
From hurt that felt real
Based on confused assumptions
And someone else's presumptions
Released on reaction
Resulting in grief momentum gaining traction.

Blinders off
Clarity rains
Over the pain
Watered down wings don't fly as well
But I'll crawl out of this unfolding hell
Dots will connect
Realizations unearthed
Soaring forward
Knowing my worth

Lead by example
On my own two feet
Everything happens for a reason.

This was a treat
This gift of release
The only thing holding me back
Is my own mind
In search of the truth
I keep hoping to find.
But people know what they know
What they chose to see
How they show up
And it might not be beside me.

I'm cutting my own rope
Because the other side is dope
Free to fly
Let the old story die
Spread wings to soar
I'm ready for more
Bigger than what was massively in my way
Creating space
Expansion in its place
Elevating my mind
And leaving that which doesn't serve me behind.

Going out to the world
With a message to stay kind
Cut the heavyweight
Start again
Clean slate
Showing up

I'll ascend
I'll elevate
Share my light
Not live with this strife
Forever Illuminate
In this life
Let's go get it!
Peace will arrive.

MULTIPLE TEMPERATURES

Giulia de Gregorio Listo

I go from blazing embers to freezing lows.
The sea which is my body moulds itself as clay
And all the elasticity of my skin seems confused.
About to break or liquify or dissolve
Because I'm never in one piece, *never completely whole.*

I'm a walking fever, bringing with me every season at once.
You could see autumn in my auburn hair,
You could see winter on the tip of my purplish fingers.

Summer comes with the heat of my passions, how I want
To do everything at the same time.
How I believe myself to own the sunlight
And the ability to keep it aflame for years.
Spring is the shy easiness that rarely happens.
Spring would be when I'm sound asleep, wanting nothing,
Dreaming of everything but at a safe distance.

I wanted a better outline.
To be certain people at the right times.
To be exclamation points throughout history and not
Just *exploited commas* that are never sure about where to land,
Nor if they really matter.

Do people really pause and breathe for a moment for me?
Do their tongues reach the top of their mouths before they
Jump to the following page, and the following name, the following
poem,
The following temperature, the following season?

Maybe that's why I want so badly to be everything, altogether.
To be silent and loud and monochrome and colourful
Before the next stanza reaches me.

That is why I reach every high and every low, never stabilizing
Or becoming something concise.
Balanced by the indeterminable.
I rejoice in the inadequacy of being multiple things.
Of seeing thousands of stars atop of my heart
Beating and exploding and recreating the world,
Not knowing who I'll wake up to be,
Nor which degree my new body will be at,
But expecting to set fire on everything I place my hands,
Only to leave with a frosty twist of events.

PARENTING PLAN FOR THE AMERICAN DREAM
Parabolical

She raged out the door screaming "I hate you! I'm never coming back! I hate you!"

I gave her a coy smile and nod, and continued reading. The smile was to annoy her, but the newspaper was of legitimate interest. You see, this is the fifth time in as many months that she's run away, and the thousandth time she has said those words. She runs to her friends house and then returns tomorrow morning. I love her, don't get me wrong. This is just part of my parenting plan.

You see, fifteen years ago when the little crying brown haired, brown eyed human, whom we named Chelsea, was born, I set out with a plan to prepare her for this world. Given current societal pressures, I couldn't engage the plan fully in the first five years, because it would be misunderstood and I'd be in jail. The day she turned five, though, it began. I started by withdrawing when she wanted me. At six I would ignore her requests for items. At seven I would purposely annoy her. At eight I began making her work for allowance. At nine I began to work more so that I wouldn't be around at home much. At ten I began pressuring her about grades at school. At eleven I stopped cooking for her. At twelve I stopped shopping for her. At thirteen I stopped all physical affection. At fourteen I started charging her rent. And now at fifteen I removed her access to the internet.

She's fifteen and five months now. I'm so proud of her. She's exactly who I dreamed she would be. And she's more than ready for the world. I thought I was independent, but now I'm learning from her. She hasn't quite been willing to fully sever ties yet, and move out on her own, but she is leaving once a month like she did just now. It's really great to watch. The plan for next year should finish the process. I'll completely stop talking to her.

It's so sad to watch all these people in the world live under an addiction to love and others. It's the drug that does the most damage to the world. You have to take what you want in this world. Nothing is given to you. You have to make your way, and success is by you being able to support and stand by yourself. I've told Chelsea these things every day of her life.

I'm thinking of starting a support group for dads against love, once she moves out for good, because I know how hard it can be to walk this path. There were so many times where everything in me wanted to embrace and help her. It's times like that, when you need support the most. There's no way I could've done this by myself. It was through the help of many people that I am where I am today with such a great daughter. But hopefully my story can encourage others that a world of independent individuals is possible.

DAFFODIL SOCIETY

Jenny N. Olson

The morning sun warms my face as I sit wrapped in a blanket.
My hair is warm to the touch and I close my eyes.

The first coffee of spring on a three season porch is a ritual,
that stimulates the soul.
Only those who have experienced the ecstasy of waking
from a deep hibernation, will understand the *tingling of my
senses.*

**New growth peeks out of the ground trusting a tantric path of
divine timing.** *Nature.*
Providing a gentle reminder of what's important on the human
egos journey.

My ego holds onto beliefs chosen like sea shells.
She carries a bag filled with emotional reactions dependent on
outside influences.
I will no longer travel weighed down by her itinerary.
I unpack these burdens and shed her layers.

I remove my blanket and absorb the spring sunshine.
I feel lighter and exposed. Vulnerable to the elements.
Pulsating and alive.
Ready to fly. Unable to move.
Seduced by words and chords of acoustic guitars…

I flirt with life who responds to my energy pulling me closer,
whispering words only my soul can interpret.

I smile at the beauty of this native language, leading my ego-free body
on its inherent crooked path.

A metamorphosis after the winter stripped me bare.

The ego will return tempting me with shiny objects,
doubting my worth, as soul sucking enigmas do.

But my devotion to nature's society of daffodils has begun.
My body and soul now joined, I surrender to a new timeline.
One where I grow *as if nobody's watching.*

AUTUMN, MIDWEST
Rachel B. Baxter

Let me breath the sweet pine air
While the non-evergreen trees
Change to colors of flame-
Here, I am more me than
I could ever hope to be,
Midwest Autumn breeze
Surrounding me-
Burning leaves,
Acorn debris,
Cracked pumpkin and
Dry marigold seeds.
The world around changes
At blinding speed,
Everything grows old and dies
From my car to the fireflies,
But year after year,
I come here to know that
The sound of the leaves
Crushing beneath my feet
Is just the same as it was
When I was but a little thing.
And year after year,
I'll begin to see my breath
Rise like smoke from my mouth
As I exhale my uncertainty and
Let it be a part of everything.

IN THE IN-BETWEEN

In-between the what
Michael Stang

Shinning is the start of pure brilliance say
the masters and the unordained an ending such as sweet,
but those peaks fathomed reached do not dwell in the valley
where consequences demand their pay.

In powder rows nothing grows I refrained.

In the in-between, time is my enemy
sounds are board-less useless expression, *locution demented*
they tire of my inability
rock mouthed I hold a pen of dust I have lost the key in sand.

Epics slip through fingers weak until they are not
now I can seem in the in-between reflections off the summits —
birthright translator of the immortals.

The pretty picture the long slow sigh of relief
followed down to the valley portals.

CONSUMPTION
Slow and painful
Noha Medhat

Poison in human form,
A nightmare's dream reborn.
That's what you are,

And it never looked so good.
The taste of destruction
Fresh on your lips,
And consume it I did,
Hit after hit.

If I could stop thinking about you
I would,
But you're the warden of my mind,
The breath on my pillow.

You're inexhaustible exhaustion,
A pack of cigarettes
With a jagged edge
And a pile of coffins.

You're the color of insanity,
Screaming red,
With black highlights
Of pain and dread.

And yet,
Stay away I didn't,
I sipped and sipped,

I let you in drip by drip.

I touched the knife and
Oops, It slipped,
Now I'm dead within your grip.

SENSATION

Rebeca Ansar

Where is the light?

Grab Despair by her pallid wrists and pull
her into the world of the living.

There is a blindfold called Plan
that has dimmed the stars in my eyes.

Where is the sound?

I long to hear in my own voice
the passionate rendition of words
carefully selected by the poet
who sits at the center of my amygdala.

Where is the touch?

If it is pain alone that will shake this numbness
from my body, then break my heart
and bring me to my knees.

Let me feel my human make.

Where is the taste?

Find me a mouth with words I can savor.
Make them a mirror to show me my soul.

And as for the scent ~

Jasmines roped together to hang from my hair.
The fragrance reminds me I too was once a girl.

I want to start from there.

SONG FOR A DROWNED MOTHER

Harry Hogg

At the edge of the ocean, where moon-flowers drip silver rain. That's where she is. A mother, dead beneath shipless waves, spreading her light in blues and insolent greens on faraway beaches.

She plays there with girls and boys, calling them all *dear heart.* Smiles brighten and break. Tears squeak in the sand.

I cannot be touched with words anymore. Only visions work. Nudity covered and clothed in rainbows, flowers, and the sea.

Don't talk to me of priests and cathedrals. Speak to me, instead, of pebbles and seaweed and hair flying in the undersea salon where she fixes her hair. Speak of leviathans and children in bright fields that rock and roll. The fishermaid and the pirate song.

A mother who drifts with ancient insanities in a place before history or religion.

I am left to stand against the fall of snow, to live outside her world, listening to lovesick songs.

Tears start. Tinklings vibrate in my chest. Long to be close, I cannot, but each morning I kiss the summer dawn of every new day without her.

It is trickery to die, yet dance on. Never to whither like the dying of flowers, but smell always like the ocean. Yes, it is trickery to leave, go hide, become nature.

I have waited so long that I have forgotten my fear and regret.

Remember this tune, so gentle and so free, notes spreading themselves out where madness exists and voices speak.

I'm the abandoned father, left on the causeway, running into the sea.

The older *dear heart* that waits on the edges of waves that bump against the sky and sand.

On all sides, I have the breadth of the globe.

The blue depths.

I should leave now. The tide is finished depositing what the ocean has discarded on today's tide and will soon be busy collecting up the sun's heat.

Among today's remnants a bottle (no note inside) and flotsam as far as can be seen along the ocean's petticoat shoreline.

Far off a dog is barking, and beyond that, I remain in the ruined kingdom of life, in a shoreline castle where I wait between the tides, writing my love to the world.

Love more satisfying than tongues entwined, bottom lips bitten, or hands holding hipbones.

I go out every high tide, not hoping to find her, but to make sure no one else does.

She was beautiful, you see.

HALLELUJAH FOR MUSIC AND POETRY
Embracing the rhythm and depths of heart and soul
Leah J.

Spring

spiritus mundi
oh collective souls! rejoice!
we carry the prose of the universe

that universal energy
our muse of inspiration
we drink it, out of the ash

rise up from strong roots, as a cactus
sustained in the soft, spring rain
witness how sweet the sound

that shadow at morning
rays of warm light, striding behind you
proves the harmony, the sharing of the secret chord

Summer

we went on into the sunlight
drank coffee with whimsical banter
stirring life's winsome allure

past rows and rows, through the angel's hair of sunlight
melting ice cream castles in the air
no burden of care or conscience

but hold that it, my proof
waterproof, shatterproof
let it be, hold that, let it be

Fall

shadow at evening
rising to meet you
the violet, evening hour that strives towards close

fairy tales, hyperboles, turn conundrums
just another dazzling circus show?
though I hold the facade and laugh as I fall

just don't let them know, don't
give yourself away, the bell jar will hide
just grip, it suffocates the tears and the fears

distorted dreams concrete, and schemes and surfacccrowds
won't you let it be,
why not let it shine, a little longer

does anyone hear? I whisper
though I crawl like an ant in mourning
every fair from fair sometimes declines

could it be, there is a God above
how, it remains, all I've ever learned from love
a broken Hallelujah

is there the second coming for
the baffled king, the broken lover
playing those zero sum games

this life, this concrete war such has no victory march
if the center cannot hold, where
the ceremony of innocence is drowned

I didn't want flowers,
I only wanted to lay with my hands turned up
and be utterly empty, quiet the cacophony

Winter

I heard there is a secret chord
play that, so it does please the Lord
no need, no other reason to be

oh death! do not brag thou!
I will wander not in it's shade
though fragments I have shored against my ruins, remain

accept the catcher in the rye and risk the desert dry
embrace the sun that it shines
I see the butterfly, can it save a wretch like me

Epilogue

with this horse, with no name, we move onwards
freedom is the journey to source the water
beneath the desert, dry and sandy, sleep

will it be?

heart and freedom, light with less pain
below where peace and love and water lay
we slouch towards Bethlehem, to be born

let it be

lift up your heart, can you see this light?
for the gifts we can share, a smile in the heart
say hallelujah

stay this journey, though hard
do you see the third
that walks beside you?

let it be

it is the Other, gliding wrapt in mantle and hood
that does fiddle whispered music on those strings
speaking words of wisdom

soul to soul
for all the broken-hearted people in the world,
there will be an answer

let it be

for the transformation
in the spirit of the world
let the conscious connect

beauty and the moonlight
share the space
with love and grace

let it be

no victory needed
see joy, share, show, be, reflect, embrace
a hallelujah

t'was blind, but now I see

I look at the clouds from both sides now
this truth is marching on, I say yes,

and so, it shall be

THE PHRASE
Tomasz W. Wiszniewski

——— *The phrase*

halcyon days is like unconscious seasoning,
a journalist's paprika, parched and too-red,
used for contrast and smart presentation.

You told yourself stories and dismissed the room, the elbow-to-elbow escapes, the devouring creek. / Abolished the joy, with its hard-earned jaws, its entryways bedded with embalmed trauma. / Joy the eighth and ninth wonder of the world, / and little stretches and moments in life were perfect.

Joy was something you felt
and happiness was something you wore
in the absence of joy.

You wore it so well it became you, skin inside out / blood sugar faint pendant. / Snowdrops warm in November / lushly blossomed and met plastic air, and your skin grew warm at their touch but you never could tell which side was the cold side. / Your smile never untamed, poisonous arrows / privily clearing the night of its charmed dread eyes, and streets stole the color from the sun; from the soil. / The earth a scoreboard bloat, / everywhere a crowd went full of wanting, and one starful of shattered joys too lonely for a dream 'evelop.

The crowd would tend to the mist in the ceiling
while no-shade tines poured from the lost
recesses of love's last vision.

Happiness, the great progenitor
of tombs, histories, unhallowed
payment, and all our darling curses,
our made-up words them halcyon
honeymoon and happiness.

Hell, bent, see — every word was once a made-up word.
Perhaps nothing is idyllic, but nothing is also vacancy

is beginning is creation is death is certainty

is constancy is pregnancy is life

is death is a rift in reality

is meaning

is self-

con-

struc-

ted.

Perhaps.
Nonetheless I slide into my curse
and, perhaps gone, I tell myself:
Nothing is idyllic,

idyll is the brain's vaccine

for the painful beautiful scene outside.

And these words, made n' strung, do me well
for now — tomorrow's bridges
half-dashes jutting, racked with the seed hands
hollering at the prop hand of time.

APPENDIX

INDULGING THE EDITORS

THE SEARCH
Heath Houston

I

My words came like a suicide
and washed out
like stillborn memories on the tide
I wept for you
as I bled inside

I climbed a wall and looked for you
and in that moment the wind blew
leaving me blind for days
through sand and tears
I saw stray images of nothing

I threw your name at the wind
and scattered your petals to the north
carried by weight of dreams
lighter than air, deeper than hell,
yet they echoed not

I stood in the desert atop high places
and shouted your name
while the clouds burst with rain
blooming all manner of life,
but I did not find you

My darling
  I have searched
through green hills and waste
and still you fade into the day like a dream
leaving me with dying fires
dull embers
and ash

II

From my ragged lungs
your name returned in echo
as though the wind joined my search
at last
sending sound and blood across stone

Broken, starving, I entered the City
fevered and alone but undeterred
I sought the eyes of masses
for your reflection
but I found only hope

I walked twisted streets with bare feet
haunted palace grounds in silk shroud
created effigies in the crowded sky
with eyes like yours
and watched them rise

Ancient books I read
scrolls with secrets blessed and damned
mixed blood and ink to draw your name
next to those of God
stained upon my face and hands

My darling
I have searched
through hovel meek
and grand houses of the dead
for a single breath that carries your name
but the city is blind
and deaf.

III

Against the yawning mouth of night
I called your name to the moon
and listened
for the wind and the wane
to carry back news

In the blinding light of day
I read your name in footprints
across burning sand,
and in the ice of the north
I left inuksuk to guide your way

I've carved years in lines,
frozen, burned, scarred,
on this weathered face
since I set out to find you.
Now I stand at the end on torn feet

Before ancient Yimorada, I presented myself
as told by the hands of dead men,
wise men, and veiled women with knives,
to be tested three times and found worthy,
to learn where I may find you at last.

Through the narrow passage I made my way
past the hanging corpses, the unworthy dead;
the howling sphinx, her question solved;

through walls of air and midnight flame,
past the door with no key

At last I stood in frozen Xanadu
and sang the sacred notes,
my words, my question, my desire,
rousing the Naga from the lotus baths,
to answer me in sibilant song:

*"You will find what you seek
in the faces of mothers,
the footprints of pilgrims,
the grip of a child,
the eyes of the broken-hearted,
the tears of the bereaved,
and the blood of the sacrificed*

*Only when you know this
will she appear to you."*
I bowed my head,
I understood
It was not an end I found
but a beginning.

RUNNING WITH THE WOLVES
Anna Rozwadowska

A dominant female runs the pack of hungry carnivores,
but a true wolf neither takes advantage nor hides,
when truth
of ancient forests is on her side, she will abide, she will provide,
he will abide, he will provide, abide-provide,
the sensual relationship of concurrent lovers who feed not off
each other, rather, build each other houses, shelters from
oscillations
and bread crumbs
leading one to poison; such shall not be, not with me.

What should you know about the common man?

Is there a drive to understand
3–6–9 in its purest form, triangular cohesion where Earth joins
Sun
where Sun joins Jupiter; secrets of the ether world,
they are not hidden from the sky, neither from the wolves; they
are partaking in the creation of structure;

just like you,

just like I.

Tesla once gained my trust; revealed aspirations of the grandest
kind,

that this human form could not fathom.
The oscillation, turn your head
to the conclusion point and you will see, within, the beginning of
all,
the zero precedence of what ancient sailors learned from the
depths of the sea.

It was me, all along, it was me, you could not see,
building your structure for your feet to stand, calcified the bones
for your legs to straddle, fed off my energy point 5–2–1, it shall
come,
it shall come, that we will see the other one, all in time it shall
come,
at the end where you see packs of wolves running
with their forefathers, ancient secrets of their predation,
suckling at the breast of the ones who gave it all,
for those who could have it all,
I bear it all,
truth cannot be contained.

HOME
Jess Kaisk

I had been lost, searching, drowning in
introspection
when you came along.

Not realizing I'd find myself, my home, in
another
then we promised forever.

Like a tsunami there were peaks, valleys in
us
as we grew.

Years passed happily, intricately in
time
we melded together.

We became one, opposite, the same in
ourselves
dreaming together.

We stretched ourselves, breaking apart
together
we found ourselves again.

In love we became again, no longer drowning in
anger

fear disappeared.

So we loved anew, fresh, strengthened in
revolution
renewed in our passions.

We were searching, looking, drowning in
possibilities
until we knew.

>She came with cries, smiles, searching in
>us
>her safety, security, family.

COME AWAY
Heath Houston

Come away from her hair, entangled, beautiful
joyous mess, strands of summer apple and field flowers
these are the days that make them bearable
these are the days that make them a pillar
upon which to set these shining moments in sight
not hidden, not ashamed, but showing in my face
a mien of wonders touched and life kissed,
rolled upon the tongue, tasted, swallowed,
warming the belly on dark and lonely days.

Come away from her wearing your favorite shirt
knowing she is wrapped in the transferred touch of you
wrapped in your scent, she prefers to have you next to her,
close to her, against her skin she feels something of you
in the familiar garment, perhaps a bit of dwelling essence
that she knows belongs to *her* now —
memories of belonging lay among less favorable moments,
to one day weigh more than despair.

Come away from strange cities with questionable food,
alone among the smooth babble of foreign tongues made plain
by faces wearing expressions like a shared wardrobe
of familiar clothing; the desire to get lost, be lost, stay lost,
emerging with scars of life sucked from the marrow,
licking every last drop, fearing even a moment gone to waste.
Returning home, a rekindled appreciation for the mundane,
the *ever-there-for-you* familiar.

Come away from sweetgrass and wildflowers,
the unsullied innocence in a clasp of hands,
watching the clouds slide past, flat on our backs,
love — a strange and distant thing, its echo a bird
not quite belonging to this scene, far enough away
to enjoy without fear, just us, immortal here
we could, in our shared imaginations, live forever
in our own Summer kingdom, sustained on kisses.

Come away from blue bays and green waters,
mermaids with sharp teeth and other dangers
awaiting the foolish — oh, I've had my share
and lived to tell the tale, open wounds now set to proud scars
a testament to all who view, that I have loved
in the face of a rolling black fog, I have loved
before the deadliest of jaws, undeterred, severed limbs
tied by endless hope, a familiar rope.

Come away
proud man, bright man, damaged man, hopeful man
unseal thyself.

Come away
gentle man, patient man, simple man, hurting man
and heal thyself.

Come away
discarded man, forgotten man, shoestring man, incidental man
anneal thyself.

Come away,
come away and prepare thyself,
Panglossian man,
for the next venture forth
still believing you deserve better than this.

Your next journey awaits.

TENDER

for Heath
Anna Rozwadowska

Your story behold my glory *you are mine for the touch,*
warmth glow crimson grow, fuschia in your cheeks that blushed
when they were around,

not a sound yet each one stole your voice,
heart overflowing with the loss words drained heavy rain,
heavy rain.

Oh, the misguided creature of the inner world,
create the broken bones,

their fragments are but for your taking,
there is no mistaking, you are gold Nephrite separate,
let no illusion shake your goal,
your separate self is no identity,
serene yet boiling inside your vision is simple, single,
one meant for the inkling of passion,
shared for the solemn soul who treads upon your words,
as if their life was infused to your expression.

You are expression,
reflection of the inward sun,
no being can take from you your splendour your drum,
beat forth dearest, for you owe it to you,
to bring forward your truest reflection,
inspection for the needy who understand your word

sing your song,
chain themselves to your melody,
you are no parody,
golden hue, be true to you,
your undertaking is to look forth and behold your being,
freedom as the bird's song flailing from jail cells,

calling out our name,

I am here, I am here!

THE FLOWERS WEREN'T FOR ME
Indira Reddy

A tidy little flower arrangement
eyes me with its structured sense,
as I wait in the reception,
strait-jacketed in formal clothes,
a half-centimetre smile
hovering out of politeness

i sit in clothes decorated with
holes made by anxious fingers
and hungry moths,
hair dishevelled and matted,
slack-jawed
my eyes dart like raptors,
searching for you
and hoping you don't come,
fingers and toes crossed
in the anticipation of
reversing the past

The clock strikes ten
and you're still not here,
irritation surges through —
you can't even be on time
for what you wanted to do;
good riddance, I sniff.
You come running,
five minutes late,
wiping your mouth.

I get up and nod.
Together, we enter

the lion's den awaits,
a matron whose spine
Time gave up on,
rakes me from tip to toe
with steely eyes,
i look away, only to meet
the blood red gash
that quivers on the corner of your lip,
shimmering with my pain,
my heart thunders
at fresh evidence
of my replacement

Small talk pleasantries
polished off in seconds,
the papers presented
rapidly signed and shoved away,
needing to get this over with

the matron raises her paw,
a gleaming claw thrust malevolently,
gracefully cuts me open
from sternum to navel,
i watch my guts roll out,
bleeding and yet, i don't die

We walk out, nod goodbye.
You stop at the vase of flowers
and exclaim how she would love this,
you turn looking for an answering smile,

and find calculated indifference.
You shrug and walk away

my blood flows, a mighty river,
my shoes squelch
those eyes of yours, soulful,
and much larger than you,
abjure me to fall again,
to do anything to make you happy,
but blood loss weakens me,
i stay frozen
and you leave.

REDEMPTION
The Winery at Wolf Creek
Jess Kaisk

Here I sit on the floor
glass half full and my
bottle empty

Snap peas and hummus
the crunch wakes me up
typing and writing
furiously
before my mind goes blank

Dreaming wildly I were a wanderer
flying and driving in
random directions

Taking a sip…
ahhhh, yes

My mind drifts to a place
far away

Redemption is found
on this floor that I sit
empty bottle at hand and
ink stained fingers

ALEX
Heath Houston

Part 1: Santa Monica

Looking across at you, eyes heavy, my fingers are inches from yours as we lie in ridiculous places after sliding to the floor. What did you give me? I've got words in my head but my mouth is dead, and you just laugh. The music is still throbbing from the main room.

Your fingers crawl closer to mine like a predator and still you laugh. It's infectious but the fingers have my attention. Your attack is to slide your fingertip along my finger, no longer laughing.

I look up and you are looking into my eyes with a serious bent and unknown intent. I noticed you immediately through the crowded room and the flickering lights. The girl with a Bauhaus t-shirt. I tried to talk over the noise when we were both on the couch but you just kissed me. No words, just your mouth shaping come on as you dragged me, shocked and confused, bumping elbows, beer on my shoes. I don't even know your name.

The little blue pill said sky and before I could wonder why, you dropped it on my tongue, ran your fingertip along my lips, and said swallow.

You kissed me again as if your tongue was checking I had complied. I asked your name, I remember now, but you never replied.

Every time I tried to speak you kissed me again and now we're both on the floor like melted wax, your fingers curling around mine. Captured.

"Do you like me?" you asked, eyes locked on mine.

"Yes," I managed to say.

"Do you think I'm pretty?"

"Yes. Very."

"But do you want to fuck me?"

"I don't even know you."

"My name is Alex."

PRECIPICE

Anna Rozwadowska

I stand at the precipice of *doing*, a long way from *"adiue,"*
shapeshifter into unbeknownst clouds, unsuspecting marvel
at the intercourse of salvation and decimation.

It is best that a forethought accompanies heavy decisions,
yet, neurons in the cortex are lame and have become timid,
seekers of dark corners where no one accentuates; *fear.*

Entrapment in unfolding, there is never an easy solution
to predicaments in life, petals falling from stems of roses while
beauty falls wayside, as age confronts the visage of expression.

Perhaps when letters fall from the coalition of words, writing
will cease and *being* will become of utmost importance,
until then, thirteenth century compilations line the shelves,
dusty in the corners of bookstores, grandeur of millennial
libraries;
chalk full of expressions waiting to be formed by the mouth —
of the sculptor.

Dignify yourself with the truth; the only thing that matters,
vestige and tribulation will follow you but that is, life,
conundrum,
you must sing to your own beat — voice — heard; *only by you,*
there is only you in the untold story that you keep within,
fantasy written in plain language, Universe keeps nudging at your

heart —
share, share what is yours, do not compare to the others;
they are not looking your way, life is your way, your voice *only*.

Perhaps it is the summer air, percolating to achieve splendour,
yet, how authentic are you being with yourself,
when the treasure chest is full of accomplices?

It remains a truth of wise living, testimony of the wild,
when one can hear their own voice in the breeze amidst ancient
trees —
calmness presides, understand your inner truth, *you finally
understand
your inner truth;*
how long must we wait,
for the understanding of what we must endure,
of who we really are?

A MOMENT OF MEMORY

Indira Reddy

We meet for a few precious moments
In the interstices of time,
In the fabric of the mind.
Souls converse in abstruse languages
Of desires and shared loves
Of everything and nothing.
In the shimmering pockets of memory
We hold each other tight
We revisit the land of love;
Untouched by the stain of the past
Free of rancour, of pain
Free of all expectations;
Holding carefully in cupped hands
A soft blooming bud of
A shared eternal moment

CHASING A STORM
Jess Kaisk

I sit with a mug of tea and my writing journal, pen tucked between the pages. With my long wool sweater, big, baggy grey sweats, and feet shoved into slippers I sit staring at the way the rain falls. Steadily from the lead colored sky, the sound of it hitting the stones and roof, how it trickles down over brick to land, finally, in the soil. I pile my now frizzy hair on top of my head and adjust my glasses.

I like the sound of rain, the thick wet smell of the trees and grass; how the birds flit from branch to branch, and the ducks swimming lazily in the water. It's the best time. No television, no chatter from other people, only gentle music of rain and birds. Its no wonder they make cd's of this, a slice of heaven on demand. Its not as good, as the real thing.

Closing my eyes I take in a deep breath, deep into my belly, savoring each scent of rain, soil, tree, and even my tea. Its chilly enough to bring gooseflesh to my skin, harden my nipples through my white tank, but I don't dare go inside. Instead, with eyes still closed reverently, I lift my face to the sky, enjoying the cold drops of rain and tendrils of breeze trickling my skin, dancing and undoing my hair.

How can anyone hate the rain? The sense of seclusion that wraps around you, creating your own universe. Thunder rumbles and clashes in the sky, while small, interspersed flashes of lightening grace the sky and clouds. Oh the clouds, thick and full, looking heavy with their rain. I want to whisper, "let it all out", so it would rain faster, but I'm no god or shaman to make the rain obey my humble command.

After some contemplation I give in to the urge and,

removing my socks, shoes, and sweater, step out onto the thick grass, embracing the rain like a long lost friend. Slowly and carefully, soaking up the sensations on my feet as I walk, I head toward the line of trees by the lake. I can see the fish swimming along the top of the water, their fins breaking the surface. I step onto the moss covered path, watching the tops of the trees move in the wind. For the love of movement, I arch my back, engage my thighs to stand on the balls of my feet, and sway.

That's how he found me. Barefoot, covered in rain and mud, swaying in time with the trees, my hair flying in the breeze. The look in his flashing grey eyes stopped me, the set of his jaw gave me pause. I glanced at him through the veil of my hair, taking in his demanding presence. When he moved towards me, his long, muscular legs moved over the ground with ease, the rocks or slippery wet grass almost helping him along the path. Towards me. Hands loosely at his sides, shoulders and hips moving with a masculine grace, you knew. You knew here was a man who knew who and what he was, and he had found power in that knowledge. I didn't know what he was, but I had an inkling along the back of my mind; here was a man who could match me. Power to power; passion to passion. It made me shiver. Leaving my mind blank to everything but instinct I ran, flinging my body over the ground, leaping towards the field.

I pushed the sound of his pursuit out of my mind, focused only on the line of woods ahead of me, and feeling the crush of grass underfoot. My peripheral vision was nothing but green shadows drenched in rain. The weight of him crashed into me, pulling me down to the ground as he softened my landing. Quickly rolling to my side I got back up, but he pulls me down, pinning me under all that muscle. The heat from his skin warms me, as we stare at each other, listening to our ragged breathing. It feels as if we are staring forever, memorizing the lines and angles of our faces. Leaning forward, mouth grazing mine gently, he buries his face in my neck. I hear him whisper softly, his breath sending shivers down my back, "I've finally found you."

BREATHE
Heath Houston & Anna Rozwadowska

I only recall the breath of your outgoing,
breeze through the very best of my skin,
a cool perforation,
a silent, prolonged kiss
somewhere in the dips of my body.

Casually caressing the once-shared rhythms,
trailing the ghostly scent of the intimately familiar
behind a vague sense of touch-faded photographs,
a memory gone somewhat strange now.

I dip, deep into my ambitions,
they have become murky and turbulent,
digging, digging into the trenches where I lay,
on the cold floor arms stretched wide,
waiting for the arrival of grandeur.

Waiting for the kiss of something held once,
grasping in helpless recall, the feel of it *slipping,*
sandlike, through fingers gone numb at the prospect —
held too tightly; not tight enough?

On the cold floor, arms stretched wide,
waiting for the brush of a soft breath,
faintly lingering like arrival on my flesh enmeshed,
in the fabric of me, my fluid bubbles in the intimacy.

Like a phantom limb, you touch me,
and I feel it yet through the skin you knew too much of,
woven too easily to unthread you from this fabric
without pulling loose bits of myself, along.

    A necessary sacrifice.
    A tribute to what was.
    A memory of shared sighs.
    An effigy of goodbye.

There is significance in the energy
in both our fusion and our fission,
an impression indelible, if singular,
abandoned for different theories
leaving only that mark which cannot be erased.

You and me, larger than we,
forces combined in efficacy,
hence the power of love, life,
the seclusion of the self in the breed
humanity erases memories as it speeds through time,

space moves and collects debris,
according to our brightest,
leaving only curious marks behind.

Clockwork, orange, eyes split open wide,
merciless in backward clarity,
they guide us in our undertaking —
oh, yes, you *were* breathtaking,

but I could not see beyond the illusion,
separation blinding me into confusion,
but there is a past,
pared from the present at last.

I know the two of us were one at one time,
a partial history in the making,
perhaps to be repeated in the memory of another
leaving different marks,
scratches on the surface.

THE STONE IN MY HEART
Indira Reddy & Noe

I turn myself inside out,
throw away pieces of me like chicken feed,
hoping to somehow garner
one small gesture of approbation,
but your eyes skip me

until — you snap your fingers;
I am a servant more than your daughter
you love your hounds and your horses
there is nothing left for me
I never questioned this before

but all my unquestioning love
is mutating into desperate need,
time is ticking, the hurt inside
is reaching critical mass — help stop it,
please…I don't want to be one who hates you

love and resentment are split by a fine line
I contemplate this as you demand coffee with sugar
I wonder how sugar can look like ground glass
I marvel that arsenic is perfectly tasteless
I bring your plate of hen fresh eggs — softly poached

you dismiss me indifferently, I'm but a waiter,
whom you ream seconds later, for the eggs' tepidness,
I tentatively remind you of winter's kiss,
you shatter the plate, yellow suns on the floor —

I should've remembered to warm the plate too…

late that night, you linger outside my door for the longest pause
I watch your shadow on the floor as you stand unsteady
but finally, you stumble drunk — back down the hall,
I wait, once you have fallen into your bed to sleep deeply,
I steal your pistol, your stash of gold and saddle your best horse

your clothes stink of cheap whisky and you,
but they hang too loose in all the right places,
cloaking where the moon might reveal the truth,
I venture, with my freshly sheared bob,
from the place where love lay buried to…somewhere…

the night is cool and I am free in this clear and open sky
my horse is fast, trustworthy and grateful
we race across the landscape — no border can hold us,
for countless days we travel bravely

riding by moonlight, we outpace the scrub,
soon, mountains loom, unknown terrain calms the fear —
no one here will know who I was, what I was,
I look up, the constellations show me your raised eyebrows,
pinpricks of fear-sweat bloom and freeze in the same instant

I shake my head, ghosts can hurt only if I let them…
I breathe in deep, the weight of you drops away,
wings unfurl from my soul — I am now, *just me*

life and love open their arms to me,
here in this new land with a new identity,
where most people think I am a young man,
and only my smiling bride knows otherwise

PARTAKE

Anna Rozwadowska & Erika Burkhalter

Bent in dimensions crooked little flower,
you are magnificent in how raw you become
stripped of your armour; naked, mitigated,
migratory birds start eternity, flesh unimbued,
chemistry of open air determines freedom solitude,
equations of etheric balm, space out the moon.

Wheels turning, like ferns unfurling,
the cycle of life catches us all in her cogs.

From the birth of the tender green nub,
to the spraying of feathered fronds, brown tassels at their tips,
time nips at our heels,
crying like the loon
dipped in the sundrenched shallows of the sunset,
waiting for the birth of another day.

Sometimes, we escape to see another spring.
And, sometimes, we curl in,
unsure of where to begin the next set of steps in *nature's,
intricate, dance.*

And sometimes, all that is left is to retreat and begin anew,
waltzing in the wind of a new reality.

And the spiral carries on; gathering astronomical particles,
that feed the atmosphere and the joining of souls.

And those birds, rising to the moon, their silhouettes ink black in
the pearly stream, *where do they fly?*
Will they be there when we die?
Or, when we sigh with rapture, their flutters rising,
carrying us higher and higher, until we cry, and fall again
into a new, naked, raw, identity?

Directful is the abyss, cringe at the surmise it is the final kiss;
lover's paradise, tingle, hurt, tinge, hurt, vibration, hurt,
escalation, *hurt,*
peace loved the dwellers of history, in time avocation of notes,
made into poems, made into pieces of art where creativity is
Supreme,
all being; look through your eye, see thy true-self, lift all illusion,

naked you stand, seeking appraisal for staring down your walls,
fuschia wrapped in gold leaf, leaf, leaf, praise the leaf; bellows in
nature,
creatures of brethren, confused yet solid for your appearance is
mandatory,
you soul-self is a mission, balm of frankincense and amber
rupture, you break:

it is time to partake, holi is a celebration of light being, colour
demands its force,
it is time to partake.

PERFORATION
Anna Rozwadowska & Indira Reddy

regrets crunch under my feet as I vacation in the past~

Memnosyne stings through the calluses in my skin,
nostalgia a catalyst — once forgotten nightmares
terrorise with renewed vigour;

memories take me under
as semaphore beasts await the unleashing —
I am morbid; slight satiation,
commanding frailty, stillborn power,
you have nothing on me,
reverberation in the midst of fallen flowers, maiden names;
Persephone,
never found in this disconsolate world; stitches only, are.

my eyes stuck in a mobius-Orpheus loop,
drag me to the primal sweltering depths of Tartarus,
I breathe in the quintessence of humanity — guilt,
empathy squeezes out salt crystals,
grating skin with ease,
blood pounds against darkened vision,

violent shapes of past; Thanatos, Umbria,
fear not the underneath,
the brewing of temptation in Gods crossing the immortal,
how long can you withstand Aphrodite?

omega-Alpha betaine ready to invite my thrust,
a coalition I must endure.

the past longs for me like driftwood high in the seas,
seeds of memory, candid endeavors, strike your whip
it longs for the castration of one's body;
you long for castration of one's body,

Hades' breath gifts regret,
his minions artistically align rack-and-pinion,
body and soul, pulled apart — agonisingly slow,

there is only belonging, perforation perhaps in the skin
I hear only drifting, set-your-mind-safety-net-to-zero,

loyal Elpis, stays by me, as she once did Pandora,
Ares has forsaken my limbs long ago.

I claim sanctuary at Apollo's feet, guts in hand, a privy sacrifice,
let me pass, pull me up to Gaia's bosom,
lay on sand and dissolve in oceans as prophets call forth;
coveting my salvation.

mortal whinings tire the Gods, they scoff at my plea,
I catapult through, on to the softness of Demeter's bounty,
air not aether gently soothes fibrillating heart

life flows through the earth, into my limbs, ember trickles,

treading slowly, hearing each humbling of the earth's crackle,
pay homage to the fallen, you walk to your grave;

surrounded by understanding eyes, soft smiles,
beckoning of a foreign lighthouse shining towards home,
hands ready to help, yet knowing enough to wait for its asking,
I smile, soul connection, and leap — pure ascension,
nothing escapes dissolution,
evanescence in stardust.

INDEX
(by author's last name where applicable)

ABOUT THE EDITORS

Heath Houston

Owner and Head Editor of Literally Literary and L² Media. Travels the world, writes anything, plays guitar, tries to sing, owns cats, lives in San Antonio, TX, laughs at his own jokes, world's worst typer, wants to be a real writer when he grows up.

- heath@heathhouston.net
- medum.com/@heath
- soundcloud.com/heathhouston
- twitter.com/heath_houston

Anna Rozwadowska

Poetry Editor of Literally Literary. I am a freelance writer and editor, photographer, psychic, medium, and spiritual guide. I have an M.A. in Environmental Sociology with over 15 years of professional experience in the social sciences and environment management fields.

- medium.com/@arozwadowska711
- twitter.com/AnnaRozwadowsk6

Indira Reddy

Prose Editor of Literally Literary. Writes poetry and short stories combining elements of story-telling, fantasy, horror, relationships and mental health. Loves dry humour, anime, psychology and food - all equally.

- medium.com/@yenna_solla
- twitter.com/yenna_solla

Jess Kaisk

Creator and Editor of Literally Literary. Jess is a wife and mother of two from Akron, OH. She holds a bachelors in History and Cultural Anthropology, is a yoga teacher, and small business owner. She's an avid book hoarder, hiker, gardener and herbalist.

- medium.com/JessK305